Dugald Stewart, James McCosh

Outlines of moral Philosophy

Dugald Stewart, James McCosh

Outlines of moral Philosophy

ISBN/EAN: 9783743332980

Manufactured in Europe, USA, Canada, Australia, Japa

Cover: Foto ©Thomas Meinert / pixelio.de

Manufactured and distributed by brebook publishing software (www.brebook.com)

Dugald Stewart, James McCosh

Outlines of moral Philosophy

OUTLINES

OF

MORAL PHILOSOPHY.

BY

DUGALD STEWART,

PROFESSOR OF MORAL PHILOSOPHY IN THE UNIVERSITY OF
EDINBURGH.

WITH A MEMOIR, A SUPPLEMENT, AND QUESTIONS,

BY

JAMES M'COSH, LL.D.,

PROFESSOR OF LOGIC AND METAPHYSICS, QUEEN'S UNIVERSITY IN IRELAND,
AND AUTHOR OF "THE METHOD OF DIVINE GOVERNMENT;"
"THE INTUITIONS OF THE MIND," ETC.

Ninth Edition.

LONDON:
SAMPSON LOW, MARSTON, LOW, AND SEARLE,
CROWN BUILDINGS, 188, FLEET STREET.
1876.

[All Rights reserved.]

JOHN CHILDS AND SON, PRINTERS.

PREFACE.

My principal object in this publication is to exhibit such a view of the arrangement of my Lectures as may facilitate the studies of those to whom they are addressed. In a course which employs more than five months, and which necessarily includes a great variety of disquisitions, it is difficult for a hearer to retain a steady idea of the train of thought leading from one subject to another; and, of consequence, the lectures, by assuming the appearance of detached discourses, are in danger of losing the advantages arising from connection and method. The following Outlines will, I hope, not only obviate this inconvenience, but will allow me in future a greater latitude of illustration and digression than I could have indulged myself in with propriety so long as my students were left to investigate the chain of my doctrines by their own reflections.

In the execution of this design I have attempted at the same time to state, under each head, a few fundamental principles, which I was either anxious to impress on the memory of my hearers, or which I thought might be useful to them, by relieving their attention during the discussion of a long or a difficult argument.

The branch of Moral Philosophy which relates to the Principles of Politics being less abstract than the others, I have contented myself with a simple enumeration of the most important articles treated of in the third part of my course. It is scarcely necessary for me to mention, that in this enumeration I have not aimed at anything approaching to systematical arrangement; and that in illustrating the titles it contains, I am obliged, by the term prescribed to my academical labours, to confine myself to very general sketches. As soon as my other engagements allow me sufficient leisure for such an undertaking, I shall attempt a separate course of lectures on this very extensive and difficult subject.

With respect to my general plan, those who are in the smallest degree conversant with ethical writers will perceive, that in its formation I have been guided almost entirely by the train of my own speculations. In following the order which these prescribed, I was far from proceeding on the supposition that it was likely to possess, in the opinion of the public, advantages over the arrangements already proposed; but it appeared to me reasonable to think, that a plan resulting from my own habits of thought would probably be better executed in my hands than any one, how perfect soever, suggested by the views of another.

DUGALD STEWART.

College of Edinburgh, Nov. 8th, 1793.

P.S.—Having of late carried into execution (at least in part) the design announced in the foregoing Preface, by a separate course of Lectures on Political Economy, I have omitted in this Edition of my Outlines the Articles which I formerly enumerated under that general title; substituting in their stead a few others, calculated to illustrate the peculiar and intimate connection between this department of Politics and the more appropriate objects of Ethics. The observations which these articles are meant to introduce may be useful, at the same time, in preparing the minds of Students for disquisitions, the details of which can scarcely fail to appear uninviting to those who are not aware of the important conclusions to which they are subservient.

Nov. 2nd, 1801.

CONTENTS.

LIFE AND WRITINGS OF THE AUTHOR.

INTRODUCTION.

SECT.   PAGE

I. Of the Object of Philosophy, and the Method of prosecuting Philosophical Inquiries 1
II. Application of the foregoing Principles to the Philosophy of the Human Mind 3
III. Causes of the slow Progress of Human Knowledge; more particularly of the Philosophy of the Human Mind, and of the Sciences immediately connected with it 4

SUBJECT AND ARRANGEMENT
OF THIS TREATISE.

PART I.
OF THE INTELLECTUAL POWERS OF MAN.

1. Of Consciousness 7
II. Of the Powers of External Perception 7
    ART. 1st. Of the Laws of Perception in the case of our different Senses 7
    ART. 2nd. Of Perception in general 11
III. Of Attention 14
IV. Of Conception 14
V. Of Abstraction 15
VI. Of the Association of Ideas 16
VII. Of Memory 18
VIII. Of Imagination 19
IX. Of Judgment and Reasoning 20
    1. Of Intuitive Evidence 20
    2. Of Deductive Evidence 21
X. Of Intellectual Powers or Capacities, formed by particular Habits of Study or of Business 23

CONTENTS.

SECT.		PAGE
XI.	Of certain auxiliary Faculties and Principles essential to our intellectual Improvement, or intimately connected with it	25
	1. Of Language	26
	2. Of the Principle of Imitation	27
XII.	Of the Intellectual Faculties of Man, as contrasted with the Instincts of the Brutes	28

PART II.

OF THE ACTIVE AND OF THE MORAL POWERS OF MAN.

CHAPTER I.

Classification and Analysis of our Active and Moral Powers.

I.	Of the Active Powers in general	30
II.	Of our Appetites	31
III.	Of our Desires	31
	1. The Desire of Knowledge	32
	2. The Desire of Society	32
	3. The Desire of Esteem	33
	4. The Desire of Power	34
	5. The Desire of Superiority	36
IV.	Of our Affections	37
	1. Of the Benevolent Affections	37
	2. Of the Malevolent Affections	40
V.	Of Self-love	41
VI.	Of the Moral Faculty	44
	ART. 1st. General Observations on the Moral Faculty; tending chiefly to show that it is an original principle of our nature, and not resolvable into any other principle or principles more simple	44
	ART. 2nd. Analysis of our Moral Perceptions and Emotions	47
	1. Of the Perception of Right and Wrong	48
	2. Of the Agreeable and Disagreeable Emotions arising from the Perception of what is Right and Wrong in Conduct	53
	3. Of the Perception of Merit and Demerit	55
	ART. 3rd. Of Moral Obligation	56
VII.	Of certain Principles which co-operate with our Moral Powers in their Influence on the Conduct	58
	1. Of Decency, or a regard to Character	58
	2. Of Sympathy	59
	3. Of the Sense of the Ridiculous	61
	4. Of Taste considered in its relation to Morals	61
VIII.	Of Man's Free Agency	63

CHAPTER II.

Of the various Branches of our Duty.

SECT.   PAGE

I. Of the duties which respect the Deity 65

PRELIMINARY INQUIRY INTO THE PRINCIPLES OF NATURAL RELIGION.

ART. 1st. Of the existence of the Deity 65
      1. Of the Foundations of our Reasoning from the Effect to the Cause, and of the Evidences of Active Power exhibited in the Universe .. 66
      2. Of the Evidences of Design exhibited in the Universe 70

ART. 2nd. Of the Moral Attributes of the Deity 78
      1. Of the Evidences of Benevolent Design in the Universe 78
      2. Of the Evidences of the Moral Government of the Deity 84

ART. 3rd. Of a Future State 85
      1. Of the Argument for a Future State, derived from the Nature of Mind 86
      2. Of the Evidences of a Future State, arising from the Human Constitution, and from the Circumstances in which Man is placed .. 89

Continuation and Conclusion of SECTION I. 92

II. Of the Duties which respect our fellow-creatures 93
  ART. 1st. Of Benevolence 94
  ART. 2nd. Of Justice 96
      1. Of Candour 97
      2. Of Uprightness or Integrity 99
  ART. 3rd. Of Veracity 103

III. Of the Duties which respect Ourselves 106
  ART. 1st. General Remarks on this Class of our Duties .. 106
  ART. 2nd. Of the Duty of employing the Means we possess to promote our own Happiness 107
  ART. 3rd. Of Happiness 109
      1. Opinions of the Ancients concerning the Sovereign Good 109
      2. Additional Remarks on Happiness 111

IV. Of the different Theories which have been formed concerning the Object of Moral Approbation 118

V. Of the General Definition of Virtue 119

VI. Of an Ambiguity in the words Right and Wrong, Virtue and Vice 120

CONTENTS.

SECT.		PAGE
VII.	Of the Office and Use of Reason in the Practice of Morality	121
	APPENDIX	123

SUPPLEMENT.

ART.
I.	The Method of Inquiry	126
II.	Moral Philosophy	127

PART I.

III.	Self-consciousness	127
IV.	The Muscular Sense	128
V.	The Object intuitively perceived by the Various Senses	128
VI.	Qualities of Matter	129
VII.	Our Ideas of the Primary Qualities of Matter	130
VIII.	The Various Forms of the Ideal Theory of Sense-Perception	130
IX.	The Seeming Deception of the Senses	131
X.	The Relativity of Knowledge	132
XI.	Unconscious Mental Operations	133
XII.	Abstraction and Generalization	134
XIII.	Association of Ideas	134
XIV.	Comparison, or the Faculty of Relations	135
XV.	The Aristotelian Logic	135
XVI.	Intuition	136
XVII.	Classification of the Intellectual Powers	136

PART II.

XVIII.	Division of the Mental Faculties	137
XIX.	Springs of Action and Emotions	138
XX.	Different Theories of the Nature of the Moral Faculty	138
XXI.	The Will	139
XXII.	The Theistic Arguments	139
XXIII.	The Infinite	141
XXIV.	Moral Evil	141
XXV.	The Utilitarian Theory of Morals	142
XXVI.	Justice	144
XXVII.	Benevolence as the Ultimate End with Deity	145

QUESTIONS.

Introduction		146
PART I.—The Intellectual Powers		147
PART II.—The Active and Moral Powers		150
CHAP. I.—Classification of our Active and Moral Powers		150
CHAP. II.—The Various Branches of Duty		156

THE LIFE AND WRITINGS OF THE AUTHOR.

DUGALD Stewart was born in the old College Buildings, Edinburgh, on Nov. 22, 1753. He was the son of the Rev. Dr. Mathew Stewart, an eminent geometrican, and Professor of Mathematics in the University of Edinburgh. At the age of eight he entered on his classical studies in the High School of Edinburgh, where he was distinguished for the elegance of his translations, and early acquired that love for the prose and poetical works of ancient Rome which continued with him through life. At the age of thirteen he commenced his studies in Edinburgh University, and among other classes, attended that of Logic under Finlayson, and that of Moral Philosophy under Adam Ferguson. In the former the text books employed were the "Elementa Philosophiæ" of Heineccius, the "Determinationes Ontologicæ," of De Vries, and Wynne's "Abridgment of Locke's Essay." By the two first he was made acquainted with the philosophical questions which were discussed on the Continent posterior to the publication of the system of Descartes; and from the other he caught the fresh observational spirit which Locke had awakened. From Adam Ferguson he acquired a taste for Moral Philosophy, and for the topics lying between ethics on the one hand, and jurisprudence on the other, which Ferguson, and after him Stewart, were so fond of discussing. But the thinker who influenced him most, who indeed determined his whole philosophic career, was Thomas Reid, who, in a modest and homely manner, but with great patience, shrewdness, and independence, was at that time unfolding the principles of common sense, and thus undermining the scepticism of Hume and laying a solid foundation for philosophy. Reid was Professor of Moral Philosophy in Glasgow, and thither Stewart resorted in 1771, after finishing his course in Edinburgh. In 1772, when only nineteen, he became substitute for his father in the chair of mathematics in Edinburgh; and in 1775 he was elected his assistant and successor. In 1778, on Adam Ferguson's temporary absence, he lectured for him on Morals; and in 1785, Ferguson having resigned, he was appointed to the office for which he was so specially fitted,—to the chair of Moral Philosophy in the University of Edinburgh. Lord Cockburn describes him as a Professor:—" His forehead was large and bald; his eyebrows bushy, his eyes grey and intelligent, and capable of conveying any emotion from indignation to pity, from serene sense to hearty humour, in which they were powerfully aided by his lips, which, though rather large, perhaps, were flexible and expressive. The voice was singularly pleasing; and as he managed it, a slight burr only made its tones softer. His ear both for music and for speech was exquisite, and he was the finest reader I have ever heard. His gesture was simple and elegant, though not free from a tinge of professional formality, and his whole manner that of an academical gentleman. He lectured standing from notes, which, with their successive additions, must, I suppose, have been nearly as full as his spoken words. His lecturing manner was professorial but gentlemanlike, calm and expository, but rising into greatness, or softening into tenderness, whenever his subject required it . . . To me his lectures were like the opening of the heavens . . . I felt that I had a soul . . . His noble views, unfolded in glorious sentences, elevated me into a higher world."

In his classes of Moral Philosophy and of Political Economy, or in his own house, where he kept boarders, he had under him a greater body of young men who afterwards distinguished themselves than any other teacher that we remember. Among them we have to place Lord Brougham, Lord Palmerston, Earl Russell, Francis Horner, Lord Lansdowne, Lord Jeffery, Sir Walter Scott, Sydney Smith, Thomas Brown, Thomas Chalmers, James Mill, Sir A. Alison, and many others who have risen to great eminence in politics, in literature, or philosophy; and most of these have acknowledged the benefit which they derived from his lectures, while some of them have carried out the social principles which he inculcated into practical measures.

In 1806 his political friends in the Liberal party procured for him a sinecure office with a salary of £300 a year. In 1809 he was in a precarious state of health, much aggravated by the death of a son, and he asked Dr. Brown to lecture for him. In 1810, Brown, being strongly recommended by Stewart, was appointed conjoint professor, and henceforth discharged all the duties of his office. Stewart now lived till the close of his life at Kinniel House, Linlithgowshire. Henceforth he was chiefly employed in maturing and arranging the philosophical works which he published. In 1822, he had a stroke of paralysis, from which however he partially recovered. He died June 11, 1828, and was buried in the Canongate Church-yard, Edinburgh.

He appeared as an author by the publication of the first volume of his Elements in 1792, and by his Outlines of Moral Philosophy prepared as a text-book for his class in 1793; and from that time

LIFE AND WRITINGS OF THE AUTHOR.

till his death, he gave a new work to the press every few years. His philosophical works have had a considerable, though a silent, influence in guiding and forming the thought of the Three Kingdoms, and we may add the English-speaking parts of America. They have created in many quarters a taste for philosophy where none existed before, and they have helped to keep England from falling under the influence of low sensational, materialistic, and utilitarian views. Sir James Mackintosh, writing to Stewart in 1802, speaks of the want of anything which he could call purely philosophic thinking in England; and Horner, in 1804, declares that the highest names in the estimation of those in the metropolis who felt any interest in speculative pursuits were Hobbes and Hartley. Such works as the Moral Philosophy of Paley were fitted to lower still farther, rather than elevate, this taste. It was altogether then for the benefit of English thought that Stewart became known in South Britain, where his elegant style, his crowning good sense, and the moderation of his views, recommended him to many who had imbibed as great an aversion as ever George III. had to Scotch metaphysics.

The first volume of his Elements was translated into French by Prevost of Geneva, and the other two by Peisse. His Outlines have been translated into the same tongue by Jouffroy, who prefixed a preface of great judgment and acuteness. It is a most interesting fact that when the higher metaphysicians of France, including Royer Collard, Cousin, and Jouffroy, undertook in the early part of this century the laborious task of throwing back the tide of materialism, scepticism, and atheism, which had swept over their land, they called to their aid the sober and well-grounded philosophy of Reid and Stewart.

His works, including his Lectures on Political Economy, published posthumously, have been collected in a valuable edition, superintended by Sir W. Hamilton, with an excellent Memoir of the Author, by Prof. Veitch. In this we have first his "Dissertation concerning the Progress of Metaphysical, Ethical, and Political Philosophy since the Revival of Letters in Europe," containing a history of modern philosophy, particularly valuable for the account of British Philosophy, but very defective in the review of Kant, whose works he knew only from translations and imperfect compends, and whose philosophy he greatly undervalued. We have next the "Elements of the Philosophy of the Human Mind," in which he unfolds the various faculties of the mind; in the second volume explaining the nature of the fundamental laws of belief, and giving his views of Logic; and in the third volume treating of such concrete subjects as the varieties of intellectual character, and of the peculiarities of the metaphysician, the mathematician, the poet, and the sexes. The "Philosophical Essays" follow, and discuss, among other miscellaneous topics, Locke's Philosophy and the nature of Beauty. The next two volumes are on the "Philosophy of the Active and Moral Powers," and are an expansion of his Outlines. We have in other two volumes his Lectures on Political Economy. We have finally his Memoirs of Adam Smith, Robertson, and Reid, containing the best accounts that we have of these eminent men, with many valuable criticisms and philosophical reflections.

Among these works the "Outlines of Moral Philosophy," are peculiarly valuable, inasmuch as they contain in a condensed form the principles which he has unfolded and illustrated in his various philosophical treatises. In some of his other works he is deficient in directness of statement, and is too diffuse and general; but in this little treatise he has compressed his thoughts, so characterized by the ripeness of wisdom, within as brief a compass as is consistent with clearness, which, I may add, is a pre-eminent excellence of the work. It is one of the best text-books of mental and moral science ever written. It has not been superseded, it has not even become antiquated. To bring it up to the times it needs only a few Supplementary Notes introducing the student to discussions which have been brought into prominence by such eminent men as Kant, Sir W. Hamilton, and Mr. J. S. Mill.

OUTLINES

OF

MORAL PHILOSOPHY.

INTRODUCTION.

SECTION I.

Of the Object of Philosophy, and the Method of prosecuting Philosophical Inquiries.

1. ALL the different kinds of philosophical inquiry, and all that practical knowledge which guides our conduct in life, presuppose such an established order in the succession of events, as enables us to form conjectures concerning the future from the observation of the past.

2. In the phenomena of the material world, and in many of the phenomena of mind, we expect with the most perfect confidence, that in the same combinations of circumstances the same results will take place. The laws which regulate the course of human affairs are investigated with much greater difficulty : but even in this class of events such a degree of order may frequently be traced as furnishes general rules of great practical utility; and this order becomes the more apparent in proportion as we generalize our observations.

3. Our knowledge of the laws of nature is entirely the result of observation and experiment; for there is no instance in which we perceive such a necessary connection between two successive events, as might enable us to infer the one from the other by reasoning *à priori*. We find from

experience that certain events are invariably conjoined, so that when we see the one we expect the other; but our knowledge in such cases extends no further than to the fact.

4. To ascertain those established conjunctions of successive events which constitute the order of the universe,—to record the phenomena which it exhibits to our observation,—and to refer them to their general laws, is the great business of philosophy.—Lord Bacon was the first person who was fully aware of the importance of this fundamental truth.—The ancients considered philosophy as the science of *causes;* and hence were led to many speculations, to which the human faculties are altogether incompetent.

5. The ultimate object of philosophical inquiry is the same which every man of plain understanding proposes to himself, when he remarks the events which fall under his observation, with a view to the future regulation of his conduct. The more knowledge of this kind we acquire, the better can we accommodate our plans to the established order of things, and avail ourselves of natural powers and agents for accomplishing our purposes.

6. The knowledge of the philosopher differs from that sagacity which directs uneducated men in the business of life, not in kind, but in degree, and in the manner in which it is acquired. 1st, By artificial combinations of circumstances, or, in other words, by *experiments*, he discovers many natural conjunctions which would not have occurred spontaneously to his observation. 2ndly, By investigating the general Laws of Nature, and by reasoning from them synthetically, he can often trace an established order where a mere observer of facts would perceive nothing but irregularity.—This last process of the mind is more peculiarly dignified with the name of *Philosophy;* and the object of the rules of philosophizing is to explain in what manner it ought to be conducted.

7. The knowledge which is acquired of the course of Nature by mere observation is extremely limited. and extends only to cases in which the uniformity of the observed phenomena is apparent to our senses. This happens, either when one single law of nature operates separately, or when different laws are always combined together in the same manner. In most instances, however, when different laws

are combined, the result varies in every particular case, according to the different circumstances of the combination; and it is only by knowing what the laws are which are concerned in any expected phenomenon, and by considering in what manner they modify each other's effects, that the result can be predicted.

8. Hence it follows, that the first step in the study of Philosophy is to ascertain the simple and general laws on which the complicated phenomena of the universe depend. Having obtained these laws, we may proceed safely to reason concerning the effect resulting from any given combination of them.—In the former instance, we are said to carry on our inquiries in the way of *Analysis;* in the latter, in that of *Synthesis.*

9. To this method of philosophizing (which is commonly distinguished by the title of the Method of Induction), we are indebted for the rapid progress which physical knowledge has made since the time of Lord Bacon. The publication of his writings fixes one of the most important eras in the history of science.—Not that the reformation which has since taken place in the plan of philosophical inquiry is to be ascribed entirely to him: for although he did more to forward it than any other individual, yet his genius and writings seem to have been powerfully influenced by the circumstances and character of the age in which he lived; and there can be little doubt that he only accelerated an event which was already prepared by many concurrent causes.

SECTION II.

Application of the foregoing Principles to the Philosophy of the Human Mind.

10. The reformation in the plan of philosophical inquiry which has taken place during the last two centuries, although not entirely confined to physics, has not extended in the same degree to the other branches of science; as sufficiently appears from the prevailing scepticism with respect to the principles of metaphysics and of moral philosophy. This scepticism can only be corrected by applying to these subjects the method of induction.

11. As all our knowledge of the material world rests ultimately on facts ascertained by observation, so all our knowledge of the human mind rests ultimately on facts for which we have the evidence of our own consciousness. An attentive examination of such facts will lead in time to the general principles of the human constitution, and will gradually form a science of mind not inferior in certainty to the science of body. Of this species of investigation, the works of Dr Reid furnish many valuable examples.

12. The objections which have been stated by some writers of the present age to the conclusions of those metaphysicians who have attempted to apply the method of induction to the science of mind, are perfectly similar to the charge which was at first brought against the Newtonian doctrine of gravitation, as being a revival of the occult qualities of the Aristotelians.—In all our inquiries, whether they relate to matter or to mind, the business of philosophy is confined to a reference of particular facts to other facts more general; and our most successful researches must always terminate in the discovery of some law of nature, of which no explanation can be given.

SECTION III.

Causes of the slow Progress of Human Knowledge; more particularly of the Philosophy of the Human Mind, and of the Sciences immediately connected with it.

13. Some of the chief of these may be referred to the following heads.

(1.) The imperfections of language, both as an instrument of thought and a medium of communication.

(2.) Mistakes about the proper object of philosophy, and the method of prosecuting philosophical inquiries.

(3.) A disposition to grasp at general principles, without submitting to the previous study of particular facts.

(4.) Difficulty of ascertaining facts, particularly in the sciences immediately connected with the philosophy of the human mind.

(5.) The great part of life which is spent in making useless literary acquisitions.

(6.) Prejudices arising from a reverence for great names, and from the influence of local institutions.
(7.) A predilection for singular or paradoxical opinions.
(8.) A disposition to unlimited scepticism.

SUBJECT AND ARRANGEMENT OF THIS TREATISE.

1. The object of Moral Philosophy is to ascertain the general rules of a wise and virtuous conduct in life, in so far as these rules may be discovered by the unassisted light of nature, that is, by an examination of the principles of the human constitution, and of the circumstances in which man is placed.

2. In examining the principles of our constitution with this view, our inquiries may be arranged under three heads; according as they refer,
(1.) To the intellectual powers of man.
(2.) To his active and moral powers. And
(3.) To man, considered as the member of a political body.

3. Of these articles, the two first coincide with the common division of human nature into the powers of the Understanding and those of the Will; a division of great antiquity, and which (abstracting from the effects of political institutions) exhausts the whole of Moral Philosophy. As man, however, excepting in his rudest state, has been always found connected with a political community, the principles which lay the foundation of this species of union may be regarded as universal and essential principles of our constitution; and, without an examination of them, it is impossible for us to have a just idea of our situation in the world, and of the most important duties we owe to our fellow-creatures. This last branch of the subject has, besides, a more intimate connection with the other two than might at first be apprehended: for it is in the political union, and in the gradual improvement of which it is susceptible, that nature has made a provision for a gradual development of our intellectual

and moral powers, and for a proportional enlargement in our capacities of enjoyment; and it is by the particular forms of their political institutions, that those opinions and habits which constitute the *Manners* of nations are chiefly determined. How intimately these are connected with the progress and the happiness of the race will appear in the sequel.

4. An investigation of the Pleasures and Pains of which we are susceptible, might furnish the subject of a fourth view of man, considered as a sensitive being. But, instead of aiming at so great a degree of analytical distinctness, it will be found more convenient to incorporate this part of the Philosophy of the Human Mind with the other three which have been already defined; connecting whatever remarks may occur on our enjoyments or sufferings, with those intellectual or moral principles, from the exercise of which they respectively arise.

PART I.

OF THE INTELLECTUAL POWERS OF MAN.

The most important of these are comprehended in the following enumeration:
 (1.) Consciousness.
 (2.) Powers of external perception.
 (3.) Attention.
 (4.) Conception.
 (5.) Abstraction.
 (6) Association of ideas.
 (7.) Memory.
 (8.) Imagination.
 (9.) Powers of judgment and reasoning.

5. Besides these intellectual faculties, which in some degree are common to the whole species, there are other more complicated powers or capacities, which are gradually formed by particular habits of study or of business. Such are, the Power of Taste; a Genius for Poetry, for Painting, for Music, for Mathematics; with all the various intellectual

habits acquired in the different professions of life. To analyze such compounded powers into the more simple and general principles of our nature, forms one of the most interesting subjects of philosophical disquisition.

6. To this branch of our constitution may also be referred those auxiliary faculties and principles, which are essential to our intellectual improvement, or very intimately connected with it; in particular, the faculty of communicating our thoughts by arbitrary signs, and the principle of imitation.

SECTION I.

Consciousness.

7. This word denotes the immediate knowledge which the mind has of its sensations and thoughts, and, in general, of all its present operations.

8. Of all the present operations of the mind, Consciousness is an inseparable concomitant.

9. The belief with which it is attended has been considered as the most irresistible of any; insomuch that this species of evidence has never been questioned: and yet it rests on the same foundation with every other kind of belief to which we are determined by the constitution of our nature.

10. We cannot properly be said to be conscious of our own existence; our knowledge of this fact being necessarily posterior, in the order of time, to the consciousness of those sensations by which it is suggested.

11. From Consciousness and Memory we acquire the notion, and are impressed with a conviction, of our own personal identity.

SECTION II.

Of the Powers of External Perception.

ARTICLE FIRST.

OF THE LAWS OF PERCEPTION IN THE CASE OF OUR DIFFERENT SENSES.

12. Our external senses are commonly reckoned to be five in number, and the same enumeration has been adopted

by the soundest philosophers. An attempt has been made by some writers to resolve all our senses into that of feeling; but this speculation has plainly proceeded from over-refinement, and has no tendency to illustrate the subject of inquiry.

13. Of our five senses there are two, viz., Touch and Taste, in which there must be an immediate application of the object to the organ. In the other three, the object is perceived at a distance, by the intervention of a material medium.

14. In order to form an accurate notion of the means by which we acquire our knowledge of things external, it is necessary to attend to the distinct meanings of the words *Sensation* and *Perception*. The former expresses merely that change in the state of the mind which is produced by an impression upon an organ of sense (of which change we can conceive the mind to be conscious, without any knowledge of external objects); the latter expresses the knowledge we obtain, by means of our sensations, of the qualities of matter.—An indiscriminate use of these two words has introduced much confusion into philosophical disquisitions.

SMELLING, TASTING, AND HEARING.

15. The qualities perceived by smelling, tasting, and hearing, are known to us only as the causes of certain sensations; and have therefore been contradistinguished by the name of *secondary qualities*, from those of which we learn the nature directly and immediately from the sensations with which they are connected. Of this last kind are extension and figure;—to which (along with some others) philosophers have given the title of the *primary qualities* of matter.

16. Abstracting from our other organs of perception, smelling, tasting, and hearing, could give us no information concerning external objects.

17. Any one of these senses, however, might suggest to the mind (or furnish the occasions of our forming) the simple ideas or notions of number, time, causation, existence, personal identity, and many others.

TOUCH.

18. The sense of Touch is spread over the whole surface of the body; but the hand is more particularly appropriated to this mode of perception; in consequence, partly, of its anatomical structure, and, partly, of the greater degree of attention we give to the impressions which are made on it.

19. Some of the qualities perceived by this sense are primary, others secondary.—In all its different perceptions, however, there is one common circumstance; that we are not only made acquainted with the existence of some quality or other, but with the particular part of the body to which the external object is applied. It is probably owing to this that we refer to Touch a variety of sensations which have little or no resemblance to each other; *heat, itching, pain,* &c. All of these suggest to us the local situation of their exciting causes; and hence we refer them to the same class.

20. The hand is useful in two respects: 1. For examining the properties of bodies, and the laws of the material world; of which properties and laws none of our other senses, unassisted by that of Touch, could convey to us any accurate knowledge. 2. For the practice of the mechanical arts.—The advantages we derive from it in these respects are so great, that some philosophers, fond of paradoxical opinions, have ascribed to it entirely our intellectual superiority over the brutes.

21. The importance of this organ to man sufficiently intimates the intentions of nature with respect to his ordinary posture; and affords a refutation of those theories which attempt to class him with the quadrupeds.

SIGHT.

22. The description of the eye, and of the manner in which the pencils of rays, proceeding from the different points of a visible object, are collected by the refractive powers of the humours, so as to form a picture on the retina, belongs properly to optics; but there are many questions arising from this subject, which are intimately connected with the philosophy of the human mind, and which optical

writers have in vain attempted to resolve on the common principles of their science. Such are all the questions that relate to the most simple and general laws of vision. These laws are *facts* which the optician must assume as the groundwork of his reasoning; not *difficulties* which he is called on to explain.

23. Among the phenomena of vision, more immediately connected with the philosophy of the human mind, the most important are those which depend on the distinction between the *original* and the *acquired* perceptions of sight. Prior to experience, all that we perceive by this sense is superficial extension and figure, with varieties of colour and of illumination. In consequence, however, of a comparison between the perceptions of sight and of touch, the visible appearances of objects, together with the correspondent affections of the eye, become signs of their tangible qualities, and of the distances at which they are placed from the organ. In some cases our judgment proceeds on a variety of these circumstances combined together; and yet so rapidly is the intellectual process performed, that the perception seems to be perfectly instantaneous.

24. This distinction, between the original and the acquired perceptions of sight, leads to an explanation of many curious phenomena, which had long puzzled those opticians who confined their attention to the mathematical principles of Dioptrics. But to the student of moral philosophy it is interesting, chiefly, as it affords a palpable and an acknowledged proof, that the mind may carry on intellectual processes which leave no trace in the memory.

25. Two other celebrated questions concerning vision are intimately connected with the philosophy of the mind, and furnish a favourable opportunity for illustrating the limits which nature has prescribed to our inquiries on the subject of perception. The one relates to our seeing objects erect, by means of inverted images on the retina; the other, to our seeing objects single with two eyes.

26. Some of the qualities perceived by sight are primary, others secondary. Extension and figure belong to the former class; colour and varieties of illumination, to the latter.

27. The foregoing article naturally leads the attention to the general accommodation of our animal frame to our intellectual faculties. Under this head the following particulars may furnish matter for useful reflections.

(1.) The local distribution of our organs of sense.

(2.) The adaptation of our perceptive powers to the properties and laws of the material world.

(3.) The relation of the stature and strength of man to the physical arrangements on that planet with which he is connected.

(4.) The versatility of his nature; qualifying him to subsist in every variety of climate.

SECTION II.

Of the Powers of External Perception.

ARTICLE SECOND.

OF PERCEPTION IN GENERAL.

28. Our notions both of body and of mind are merely relative; that is, we can define the former only by the qualities perceived by our senses, and the latter by the operations of which we are conscious.

29. As the qualities of body bear no resemblance to the operations of mind, we are unavoidably led to consider them as perfectly distinct objects of our knowledge; each of which must be studied in its own peculiar way: The one by attention to the subjects of our consciousness; the other by attention to the objects of our perceptions.—This is not a hypothesis, but a fact, which is implied in the only notions of body and of mind that we are capable of forming.

30. It appears, however, from the phenomena of perception, and also from those of voluntary motion, that the connection between body and mind is extremely intimate; and various theories have been proposed to explain the manner in which it is carried on. All these theories relate to a subject placed beyond the reach of our faculties; concerning which it is impossible for us to ascertain anything, but the laws by which the connection is regulated.

31. According to the distinction formerly stated between

the primary and the secondary qualities of matter (15.), our notions of the latter are merely relative; the sensations which correspond to them informing us of nothing but of the existence of certain unknown causes by which they are produced. What we know of the nature of these causes is the result of subsequent philosophical investigation.—The names of secondary qualities are in all languages ambiguous; the same word expressing the sensation, and the unknown cause by which it is excited. Hence the origin of the Cartesian paradox with respect to the non-existence of heat, cold, smell, sound, and colour.

32. The primary qualities of matter (such, for example, as extension and figure), although perceived in consequence of certain sensations excited in our minds, are always apprehended as external and independent existences; and the notions of them we form have in general no reference to the sensations by which they are suggested. The truth seems to be, that these sensations were intended by nature to perform merely the office of signs, without attracting any notice to themselves; and as they are seldom accompanied either with pleasure or pain, we acquire an habitual inattention to them in early infancy, which is not easily to be surmounted in our maturer years.

33. As our sensations have no resemblance to the qualities of matter, it has puzzled philosophers to explain in what manner our notions of primary qualities are acquired. It is this difficulty that has given rise to the modern scepticism concerning the non-existence of matter.

34. According to the ancient theory of perception, sensible qualities are perceived by means of images or species propagated from external objects to the mind, by the organs of sense. These images (which since the time of Descartes have been commonly called *Ideas*) were supposed to be resemblances of the sensible qualities; and, like the impression of a seal on wax, to transmit their form without their matter. This hypothesis is now commonly distinguished by the title of the Ideal Theory.

35. On the principles of this theory, Berkeley demonstrated that the existence of matter is impossible: for, if we have no knowledge of anything which does not resemble our ideas or sensations, it follows that we have no knowledge

of anything whose existence is independent of our perceptions.

36. If the Ideal Theory be admitted, the foregoing argument against the existence of matter is conclusive; but the theory is unsupported by evidence, and is even inconceivable. That we *have* notions of external qualities perfectly unlike to our sensations, or to anything of which we are immediately conscious, is a *fact;* nor ought we to dispute the reality of what we perceive, because we cannot reconcile this fact with our received philosophical systems.

37. Dr Reid, who first called the Ideal Theory in question, offers no argument to prove that the material world exists, but considers our belief of it as an ultimate fact in our nature.—It rests on the same foundation with our belief of the reality of our sensations, which no man has disputed.

38. Beside the Ideal Theory, other attempts have been made to explain in what manner the communication between mind and matter is carried on, in the case of perception.— Leibnitz's system of pre-established harmony, taking for granted the impossibility of any immediate connection between two substances essentially different, represents the human mind and human body as two independent machines, adjusted at their first formation to an invariable correspondence with each other, like two clocks made to correspond in all their movements.—By means of the same hypothesis he endeavoured to account for the phenomena of Voluntary Motion.

39. The following are the most important general laws of our perceptions, as far as we can infer them from acknowledged facts.

(1.) The object, either immediately, or by means of some material medium, must make an impression on the organ.

(2.) By means of the organ, an impression is made on the nerves.

(3.) By means of the nerves, an impression is made on the brain.

40. With respect, however, to the manner in which this process is carried on, and even with respect to the nature of the changes that take place in the nerves and brain, in the case of perception. we are hitherto ignorant; nor does there

seem to be any probability that we shall ever obtain satisfactory information. Physiologists, as well as metaphysicians, have, in this instance, too frequently lost sight of the just rules of philosophizing, and have proposed many conjectures which afford no explanation of the phenomena in question, and which have sometimes led to dangerous conclusions.

SECTION III.

Of Attention.

41. It appears from the acquired perceptions of sight that a process of thought may be carried on by the mind without leaving any trace in the memory; and many facts prove that impressions may be made on our organs of sense, and yet be forgotten next moment. In such cases our want of recollection is ascribed, even in ordinary conversation, to a want of *attention;* so that it seems to be a principle sufficiently ascertained by common experience, that there is a certain act or exertion of the mind necessary to fix in the memory the thoughts and the perceptions of which we are conscious. This act is one of the simplest of all our intellectual operations, and yet it has been very little noticed by writers on pneumatology.

42. Having established the certainty of the general fact by an induction of particulars, we are entitled, by all the rules of sound philosophizing, to employ it as a principle for the explanation of other phenomena. Many very curious ones, which are commonly referred to other causes, are resolvable into this principle, in a manner equally simple and satisfactory.

SECTION IV.

Of Conception.

43. The lower animals, as far as we are able to observe, are entirely occupied with their present sensations and perceptions; but man is possessed of a faculty by which he can *represent* to himself sensations of which he has been formerly conscious, and external objects which he has form-

erly perceived. This faculty may be conveniently distinguished by the name of Conception.

44. The objects of some senses are more easily conceived than those of others; above all, the objects which are perceived by the eye. The power of conception, however, may, in the case of all our senses, be greatly improved by experience.

45. It is commonly understood that conception is accompanied with no belief of the existence of its objects; but various considerations render this opinion somewhat doubtful.

46. This faculty has obviously a very intimate connection with the body. The conception of a pungent taste produces a rush of saliva into the mouth. The conception of an instrument of torture applied to any member of the body produces a shock similar to what would be occasioned by its actual application.

SECTION V.

Of Abstraction.

47. By our perceptive powers we are made acquainted only with what is *particular* or *individual;* but this description comprehends a very small part of the subjects about which our thoughts are employed. In by far the greater number of instances, our reasonings relate to classes or genera of objects or of events.

48. The process of classification supposes a power of attending to some of the qualities or circumstances of objects and events, and of withdrawing the attention from the rest. This power is called by logicians, *abstraction.* It may be defined, in more general terms, " the faculty by which the mind separates the combinations which are presented to it, in order to simplify the objects of its consideration."

49. An appellative, or a generic word, is a name applicable in common to a number of individuals, which agree with each other in some particulars and differ in others. By means of such words we are enabled to reason concerning classes of objects and classes of events, and to arrive at general conclusions, comprehending under them a multitude

of particular truths. The use which is made in algebra of the letters of the alphabet affords the best illustration of the nature of general reasoning, and of the principles on which it proceeds. These principles were long misunderstood by philosophers, who imagined that a generic word expresses an actual existence distinct from the individuals of which the genus is composed; and that the mind has a faculty of directing its attention to this general IDEA or ESSENCE, without the mediation of language. Hence much of the mystery which still prevails in the abstract sciences.

50. As it is by language alone that we are rendered capable of general reasoning, one of the most valuable branches of logic is that which relates to the use of words. Too little attention has hitherto been bestowed on this subject.

51. It is not, however, sufficient that we guard against error, in ascertaining the truth of our general principles. However accurately just they may be in themselves, considered as speculative maxims they must always be applied, in actual practice, with the utmost caution. To illustrate the advantages resulting from the proper use of them, and the mistakes produced by their abuse, would form another very important article in a philosophical system of logic.

52. A habit of abstract speculation, uncorrected by experience, and a habit of unenlightened practice, without the aid of general principles, are two opposite extremes, to which we are liable, in the conduct of the understanding. Few men are to be found, who have not acquired, in early life, a manifest bias either to the one or to the other.

SECTION VI.

Of the Association of Ideas.

53. The effect of custom in connecting together different thoughts, in such a manner, that the one seems spontaneously to follow the other, is one of the most obvious facts with respect to the operations of the mind. To this law of our constitution, modern philosophers have given the name of the Association of Ideas.—Of late the phrase has been

used in a more extensive sense, to denote the tendency which our thoughts have to succeed each other in a regular train; whether the connection between them be established by custom, or arise from some other associating principle.

54. What the different circumstances are which regulate the succession of our thoughts it is not possible, perhaps, to enumerate completely. The following are some of the most remarkable: Resemblance, Analogy, Contrariety, Vicinity in Place, Vicinity in Time, Relation of Cause and Effect, Relation of Means and End, Relation of Premises and Conclusion. Whether some of these may not be resolvable into others it is not very material to inquire.—The most powerful of all the associating principles is undoubtedly Custom; and it is that which leads to the most important inquiries of a practical nature.

55. Among the associating principles already enumerated there is an important distinction. The relations on which some of them are founded are *obvious;* and connect our thoughts together, when the attention is not directed particularly to any subject. Other relations are discovered only in consequence of efforts of meditation or study. Of the former kind are the relations of Resemblance and Analogy, of Contrariety, of Vicinity in Time and Place; of the latter, the Relations of Cause and Effect, of Means and End, of Premises and Conclusion. It is owing to this distinction that transitions, which would be highly offensive in philosophical writing, are the most pleasing of any in poetry.

56. In so far as the train of our thoughts is regulated by the laws of Association, it depends on causes, of the nature of which we are ignorant, and over which we have no direct or immediate control. At the same time, it is evident that the will has some influence over this part of our constitution. To ascertain the extent and the limits of this influence is a problem of equal curiosity and importance.

57. We have not a power of summoning up any particular thought, till that thought first solicit our notice. Among a crowd, however, which present themselves, we can choose and reject. We can detain a particular thought, and thus check the train that would otherwise have taken place.

58. The *indirect* influence of the will over the train of

our thoughts is very extensive. It is exerted chiefly in two ways: 1. By an effort of attention we can check the spontaneous course of our ideas, and give efficacy to those associating principles which prevail in a studious and collected mind. 2. By practice we can strengthen a particular associating principle to so great a degree as to acquire a command over a particular class of our ideas.

59. The effect of habit, in subjecting to the will those intellectual processes which are the foundation of wit,—of the *mechanical* part of poetry (or, in other words, of the powers of versification and rhyming),—of poetical fancy,—of invention in the arts and sciences;—and, above all, its effect in forming a talent for extempore elocution, furnish striking illustrations of this last remark.

60. Of all the different parts of our constitution, there is none more interesting to the student of moral philosophy than the laws which regulate the Association of Ideas. From the intimate and almost indissoluble combinations, which we are thus led to form in infancy and in early youth, may be traced many of our speculative errors; many of our most powerful principles of action; many perversions of our moral judgment; and many of those prejudices which mislead us in the conduct of life. By means of a judicious education, this susceptibility of the infant mind might be rendered subservient not only to moral improvement, but to the enlargement and multiplication of our capacities of enjoyment.

SECTION VII.

Of Memory.

61. The theories which attempt to account for the phenomena of Memory, by means of impressions and traces in the brain, are entirely hypothetical; and throw no light on the subject which they profess to explain.

62. This faculty appears, indeed, to depend much on the state of the body; as may be inferred from the effects of intoxication, disease, and old age. A collection of facts with respect to these effects, as they are diversified in different instances, would form a valuable addition to our knowledge, and might lead to important conclusions.

63. On a superficial view of the subject, the original differences among men, in their capacities of memory, would seem to be immense. But there is reason for thinking that these differences are commonly over-rated, and that due allowances are not made for the diversity of appearance which the human mind must necessarily exhibit in this respect, in consequence of the various walks of observation and of study to which mankind are led, partly by natural propensity, and partly by accidental situation.

64. Independent of any inequalities in the original capacity, there are remarkable *varieties* of memory, which lay the foundation of important distinctions among individuals in point of intellectual character.

65. These varieties arise chiefly from the different modes in which the constituent qualities of memory are combined in different instances. The perfection of memory is to unite Susceptibility, Retentiveness, and Readiness: but such an union is rare; and any extraordinary improvement that is bestowed on one of these qualities is generally purchased at the expense of the others.

SECTION VIII.

Of Imagination.

66. The province of Imagination is to select qualities and circumstances from a variety of different objects; and, by combining and disposing these, to form a new creation of its own. In this appropriated sense of the word, it coincides with what some authors have called *Creative* or *Poetical Imagination*.

67. This power is not a simple faculty; but results from the combination of several different ones. The effort, for example, of the painter, in composing an ideal landscape, implies Conception, which enables him to represent to himself those beautiful scenes in nature, out of which his selection is to be made;—Abstraction, which separates the selected materials from the qualities and circumstances connected with them in the memory;—and Judgment or Taste, which selects the materials, and directs their combination.

68. The nature and province of imagination are most

clearly exemplified in the arts which convey pleasure to the mind by new modifications and combinations of beauties originally perceived by the eye. The operations of imagination, in this particular instance, serve to illustrate the intellectual processes by which the mind deviates from the models presented to it by experience, and forms to itself new and untried objects of pursuit, in those analogous but less palpable cases which fall under the consideration of the moralist. It is in consequence of such processes (which, how little soever they may be attended to, are habitually passing in the thoughts of all men) that human affairs exhibit so busy and so various a scene; tending, in one instance, to improvement, and, in another, to decline; according as our notions of excellence and of happiness are just or erroneous.

SECTION IX.

Of Judgment and Reasoning.

69. Judgment is defined, by the writers on logic, to be an act of the mind by which one thing is affirmed or denied of another;—a definition which, although not exceptionable, is as good as the nature of the subject admits of.

70. In some cases our judgments are formed as soon as the terms of the proposition are understood; or they result so necessarily from the original constitution of the mind, that we act upon them, from our earliest infancy, without ever making them an object of reflection. In other cases they are formed in consequence of a process of thought, consisting of different successive steps. Hence, a distinction of *Evidence* into *intuitive* and *deductive*.

I. *Of Intuitive Evidence.*

71. The most important, if not all the different species of intuitive evidence, may be comprehended under the three following heads:

(1.) The evidence of axioms.

(2.) The evidence of consciousness, of perception, and of memory.

(3.) The evidence of those fundamental laws of human belief, which form an essential part of our constitution; and of which our entire conviction is implied, not only in all speculative reasonings, but in all our conduct as active beings. —Of this class is the evidence for our own personal identity; for the existence of the material world; for the continuance of those laws which have been found, in the course of our past experience, to regulate the succession of phenomena. Such truths no man ever thinks of stating to himself in the form of propositions; but all our conduct, and all our reasonings, proceed on the supposition that they are admitted. The belief of them is necessary for the preservation of our animal existence; and it is accordingly coeval with the first operations of the intellect.

72. The attacks of modern sceptics have been chiefly directed against this last description of intuitive truths. They have been called *Principles of Common Sense*, by some late writers, who have undertaken to vindicate their authority. The conclusions of these writers are, on the whole, solid and important: but the vagueness of the expression *Common Sense*, which is generally employed, in ordinary discourse, in a sense considerably different from that in which it was at first introduced into this controversy, has furnished to their opponents the means of a specious misrepresentation of the doctrine in question; as an attempt to shelter popular prejudices from a free examination; and to institute an appeal, from the decisions of philosophy, to the voice of the multitude.

II. *Of Deductive Evidence.*

73. Notwithstanding the commonly received doctrine concerning the radical distinction between Intuition and Reasoning, it may be doubted if the one of these powers be not implied in the other. If it be true that a perfect demonstration is constituted by a chain of reasoning, in which all the links are connected by intuitive evidence; it will follow that the power of reasoning presupposes the power of intuition. On the other hand, are not the powers of intuition and of memory sufficient to account for those processes of thought which conduct the mind by a series of consequences, from premises to a conclusion?

74. "When the mind (says Locke) perceives the agreement or disagreement of two ideas immediately by themselves, without the intervention of any other, its knowledge may be called *intuitive*. When it cannot so bring its *ideas* together, as by their immediate comparison, and, as it were, juxtaposition, or application one to another, to perceive their agreement or disagreement, it is fain, by the intervention of other ideas (one, or more, as it happens), to discover the agreement or disagreement which it searches; and this is what we call *Reasoning*."—According to these definitions, supposing the equality of two lines A and B to be perceived immediately, in consequence of their coincidence, the judgment of the mind is intuitive. Supposing A to coincide with B, and B with C, the relation between A and C is perceived by Reasoning.

75. This is certainly not agreeable to common language. The truth of mathematical axioms has always been supposed to be intuitively obvious; and the first of these, according to Euclid's enumeration, affirms that if A be equal to B, and B to C, A and C are equal.

76. Admitting, however, Locke's definition to be just, it might easily be shown that the faculty which perceives the relation between A and C is the same with the faculty which perceives the relation between A and B, and between B and C. When the relation of equality between A and B has once been perceived, A and B become different names for the same thing.

77. That the power of reasoning (or, as it has been sometimes called, the Discursive Faculty) is implied in the powers of intuition and memory, appears also from an examination of the structure of syllogisms. It is impossible to conceive an understanding so formed, as to perceive the truth of the major and minor propositions, and not to perceive the truth of the conclusion. Indeed, as in this mode of stating an argument the mind is led from universals to particulars, the truth of the conclusion must have been known before the major proposition is formed.

78. Deductive evidence is of two kinds, Demonstrative and Probable. The former relates to necessary, the latter to contingent truths. An accurate examination and comparison of these are of great consequence to all who engage

in moral inquiries. But the subject is too extensive to be introduced here.

79. The process of the mind, in discovering media of proof for establishing the truth of doubtful propositions, and also the process by which we bring new truths to light, is properly called Invention. In this power, remarkable inequalities are observable among different individuals. In a capacity of understanding the reasonings of others, all men seem to be nearly on a level.

80. The word *Logic* is used by modern writers in two very different senses: 1. To express the scholastic art of syllogizing, which is commonly referred to Aristotle for its inventor. 2. To express that branch of the philosophy of the human mind which has for its object to guard us against the various errors to which we are liable in the exercise of our reasoning powers, and to assist and direct the inventive faculty in the investigation of truth. The general aim of these two sorts of logic is the same; and they differ only in the justness of the principles on which they proceed. The inutility of the former is now pretty generally acknowledged, and it deserves our attention, chiefly, as a curious article in the history of science. The other is still in its infancy; but many important views have already been opened into the subject by Lord Bacon and others.

SECTION X.

Of Intellectual Powers or Capacities, formed by particular Habits of Study or of Business.

81. The varieties of intellectual character among men result from the various possible combinations and modifications of faculties, which, in greater or less degrees, are common to the whole species. Supposing these faculties to be originally the same in every individual, infinite diversities of genius would necessarily arise, from the different situations into which men are thrown by the accidents of human life.

82. The intellectual habits that are formed by the pursuits of science or of literature are widely different from those which are produced by the active engagements of business.

There are other peculiarities of a more delicate nature, which originate from particular studies, and which distinguish the different classes of literary men from each other. The metaphysician, the mathematician, the antiquary, the poet, the critic, strengthen, by their respective pursuits, particular faculties and principles, while they suffer others to remain without due cultivation.

83. An examination of the effects produced on the understanding, by different sciences and by different active professions, would suggest many important rules for the improvement and enlargement of the mind, and for preserving all its various powers in that just proportion to each other which constitutes the perfection of our intellectual nature.

84. Quickness, Acuteness, Penetration, Presence of Mind, Good Sense, Sagacity, Comprehension, Profoundness,—all express particular characteristics of intellect by which individuals are distinguished from each other, and which present a subject of observation and study, not more interesting to the philosopher than to those who take an active concern in the business of the world. The mental defects to which these qualities are respectively opposed are no less deserving of attention.

85. Nearly connected with these last speculations are those philosophical inquiries which have for their object to analyze, into their constituent principles, the different kinds of intellectual ability which are displayed in the different sciences and arts. Such inquiries not only open a curious and interesting field of disquisition, but have an obvious tendency to lessen that blind admiration of original genius which is one of the chief obstacles to the improvement of the arts, and to the progress of knowledge.

---

86. Among the intellectual powers, gradually formed by a particular application of our original faculties, the power of Taste is one of the most important. It was formerly treated by metaphysicians as a simple and uncompounded principle of our constitution; and notwithstanding the ingenious attempts lately made to analyze it into its component elements, it continues still to be considered by some

as an ultimate fact in the constitution of the human mind. The extensive influence it possesses in such a state of society as ours, not only over the pursuits of those who devote themselves to the study of Literature and of the Fine Arts, but over the enjoyments of every individual who partakes of the general refinement of manners, might justify the allotment of a separate article to an illustration of the intellectual process by which it is formed. Such a digression, however, would necessarily encroach on other discussions still more closely connected with the object of this First Part of the Course; and the intimate relation between the Power of Taste and our Moral Principles will furnish another and a more convenient opportunity of resuming the speculation.

87. It is sufficient, at present, to remark that although the ground-work of Taste must be laid in the original qualities of the mind, yet this power is the slow result of experience, habitually and attentively conversant with a particular class of agreeable objects. The instantaneous rapidity of its decisions gives it sometimes the appearance of an immediate perception; and hence the name which it has borrowed, in the languages of modern Europe, from one of the external senses. The use made in the French tongue of the word *Tact*, to denote that delicate sense of propriety which enables a man to *feel his way* in the difficult intercourse of polished society, seems to have been suggested by similar considerations. This power, as well as the other, is evidently an acquired one; and a comparison of the two might be useful for illustrating the nature and *genesis* of both.

SECTION XI.

Of certain auxiliary Faculties and Principles, essential to our intellectual Improvement, or intimately connected with it.

88. The form and posture of the human body, and its various organs of perception, have an obvious reference to Man's rational nature; and are beautifully fitted to encourage and facilitate his intellectual improvement. A similar remark may be extended to many other parts of our con-

stitution, both external and internal: but there are two which more particularly claim our attention,—the power of expressing our thoughts by Language, and the principle of Imitation.

I. *Of Language.*

89. The connection of this subject with that of the foregoing sections is sufficiently obvious. It is to the use of artificial signs (§ 49.) that we are indebted for all our general conclusions: and without it, our knowledge would have been entirely limited to individuals. It is also to the use of artificial signs that we are indebted for all that part of our information which is not the immediate result of our own personal experience; and for that transmission of intellectual acquisitions from one race to another, which lays the foundation of the progressive improvement of the species.

90. The formation of an artificial language (as Dr Reid has remarked) presupposes the use of natural signs. These consist in certain expressions of the countenance, certain gestures of the body, and certain tones of the voice.

91. There seems to be, in man, a power of interpreting instinctively some of these expressions. This, indeed, has been disputed of late; but various considerations might be mentioned which justify the common opinion upon the subject, when stated with certain corrections and limitations.

92. As ideas multiply, the imperfections of natural language are felt; and men find it necessary to invent artificial signs, of which the meaning is fixed by mutual agreement. In proportion as artificial language improves, the language of nature declines; insomuch that in such a state of society as ours, it requires a great deal of reflection and study to recover the use of it. This study is in a considerable degree the foundation of the arts both of the actor and of the orator.

93. Artificial signs may be divided into those which are addressed to the eye, and those which are addressed to the ear. The latter have formed, among all nations, the ordinary medium of intellectual communication.

94. As we have no record of the steps by which any of

the languages spoken among men have arisen, some writers have employed their ingenuity in tracing, from the faculties of the mind, the origin of the different parts of speech; and in illustrating the gradual progress of language resulting from the general progress of society.—Such conjectural speculations concerning the natural advances of the Species, in any particular line of improvement, may be distinguished by the title of *theoretical histories*.

95. The imperfections of those languages which have originated from popular use, have suggested, to some philosophers, the idea of a language expressly calculated for the purposes of science. The failure of the attempts hitherto made on this subject are not decisive against the practicability of such a project.

96. The art of Writing is an important step in the history of language; and a powerful aid to the intellectual progress of the species.

97. The advantages with which it is accompanied are wonderfully extended by the art of Printing, which may be justly regarded, not only as the happiest of all expedients for facilitating the intellectual commerce of mankind, but as one of the most important events that have occurred in the history of human affairs.

II. *Of the Principle of Imitation.*

98. Whenever we see any expression, or, in general, any change, in the countenance of another person; we have a tendency to assume the same expression, or the same change, in our own countenance. Every man is sensible of this when he looks at another in a rage, in a fit of laughter, or in a deep melancholy.—Nor is it the *visible* appearance alone of others, that we have a disposition to imitate. We copy instinctively the vices of our companions, their tones, their accents, and their modes of pronunciation.

99. This tendency in our nature to imitation is attended with important advantages. It seems to be by means of it that children acquire the use of speech; and that they learn, insensibly, to model their habits, on the appearance and manners of those with whom they are familarly conversant.

100. As it is in early life that the principle of imitation

is of greatest use to us, so it is in infancy that we have the strongest tendency to indulge it.—It is of this natural tendency, which all men have in some degree, that mimics avail themselves; till, by repeated efforts, they acquire a power of carrying it further than they could have done originally: or rather perhaps, they only contrive to retain through life a faculty which, in the case of most men, disappears after the period of childhood.

101. The contagious nature of insanity, of convulsions, of hysteric disorders, of panics, and of all the different kinds of enthusiasm, seems to have an intimate connection with the principle of imitation. To this class of facts an important addition has lately been made, in the course of the philosophical inquiries which took rise at Paris, in consequence of the cures pretended to be effected by means of animal magnetism.

SECTION XII.

Of the Intellectual Faculties of Man, as contrasted with the Instincts of the Brutes.

102. That the brutes are under the more immediate guidance of nature, while man is left to regulate, to a great degree, his own destiny, by the exercise of his reason, is a fact too obvious to admit of dispute. In what manner, indeed, nature operates, in this instance, we are perfectly ignorant: but nothing can be more certain than this, that it is not by a deliberate choice, analogous to what we experience in ourselves, that the lower animals are determined to the pursuit of particular ends; nor by any process analogous to our reason that they combine means in order to attain them.

103. To that unknown principle which guides the operations of the brutes, we give the name of Instinct. It is distinguished from Reason by two circumstances: 1. By the uniformity with which it proceeds in all individuals of the same species; and, 2. By the unerring certainty with which it performs its office prior to all experience.

104. But although we do not, in such cases, ascribe reason or art to the brutes, the operations of instinct plainly indicate intelligence in that Being by whom they were form-

ed; and who, by adapting their constitution so beautifully to the laws of the material world, has evinced a unity of design, which proves that all the different parts of the universe, animate and inanimate, are the workmanship of the same Author.

105. The wisdom of nature, as displayed in the instincts of animals, is more particularly conspicuous in those tribes which associate in political communities;—as the bee and the beaver. Here we see animals, who, considered individually, discover but a small degree of sagacity, conspiring together, under the guidance of a blind impulse, in the accomplishment of effects, astonishing by their magnitude and by the complicated ingenuity they exhibit.

106. Animals, however, are left to make some small acquisitions by experience; as sufficiently appears, in certain tribes, from the sagacity of the old, when contrasted with the ignorance of the young, and from the effects which may be produced on many of them by discipline and education.

107. In what, then, does the difference between man and the brutes consist? Do their faculties differ from each other in degree only; or is there an essential distinction between the rational and the animal natures?

108. The French philosophers of the Cartesian school adopted the latter opinion, and even carried it so far as to consider the brutes as mere machines. Their successors have, in general, gone into the opposite extreme, and have employed their ingenuity in attempting to account for the boasted superiority of man, by accidental circumstances in his bodily organization or in his external condition.

109. In opposition to these doctrines of modern Materialists, a great variety of considerations prove that, in respect of our intellectual and moral principles, our nature does not admit of comparison with that of any other inhabitant of this globe; the difference between our constitution and theirs being a difference, not in degree, but in kind. Perhaps this is the single instance in which that regular gradation which we, everywhere else, observe in the universe, fails entirely.—The subject is by far too extensive to be treated in these *Outlines*.

PART II.

OF THE ACTIVE AND OF THE MORAL POWERS OF MAN.

110. This part of the subject naturally divides itself into two Chapters; The first relates to the Classification and Analysis of our Active and Moral Powers. The second, to the various branches of our Duty.

CHAPTER I.

CLASSIFICATION AND ANALYSIS OF OUR ACTIVE AND MORAL POWERS.

SECTION I.

Of the Active Powers in general.

111. The word *Action* is properly applied to those exertions which are consequent on volition; whether the exertion be made on external objects, or be confined to our mental operations. Thus, we say the mind is active when engaged in study. In ordinary discourse, indeed, we are apt to confound together action and motion. As the operations in the minds of other men escape our notice, we can judge of their activity only from the sensible effects it produces; and hence we are led to apply the character of Activity to those whose bodily activity is the most remarkable; and to distinguish mankind into two classes, the Active and the Speculative.—In the present instance, the word Activity is used in its most extensive signification, as applicable to every voluntary exertion.

112. The primary sources of our activity, therefore, are the circumstances that influence the will. Of these, there are some which make a part of our constitution, and which, on that account, are called Active principles. Such are, hunger, thirst, curiosity, ambition, pity, resentment. The most important principles of this kind may be referred to the following heads.

(1.) Appetites.
(2.) Desires.

(3.) Affections.
(4.) Self-Love.
(5.) The Moral Faculty.

SECTION II.
Of our Appetites.

113. This class of our active principles is distinguished by the following circumstances.

(1.) They take their rise from the body, and are common to us with the brutes.

(2.) They are not constant but occasional.

(3.) They are accompanied with an uneasy sensation, which is strong or weak in proportion to the strength or weakness of the appetite.

114. Our appetites are three in number,—Hunger, Thirst, and the appetite of Sex. Of these, two were intended for the preservation of the individual; the third, for the continuance of the species; and without them, reason would have been insufficient for these important purposes.

115. Our appetites can with no propriety be called selfish, for they are directed to their respective objects as ultimate ends; and they must all have operated, in the first instance, prior to any experience of the pleasure arising from their gratification.—Self-love, too, is often sacrificed to appetite, when we indulge ourselves in an immediate enjoyment, which we know is likely to be attended with hurtful consequences.

116. Besides our natural appetites, we have many acquired ones.—Such are, an appetite for tobacco, for opium, and for intoxicating liquors. In general, everything that stimulates the nervous system produces a subsequent languor, which gives rise to a desire of repetition.

117. Our occasional propensities to action and to repose are, in many respects, analogous to our appetites.

SECTION III.
Of our Desires.

118. These are distinguished from our appetites by the following circumstances.

(1.) They do not take rise from the body.

(2.) They do not operate periodically, after certain intervals: and they do not cease upon the attainment of a particular object.

119. The most remarkable active principles belonging to this class are;

(1.) The Desire of Knowledge, or the Principle of Curiosity.
(2.) The Desire of Society
(3.) The Desire of Esteem.
(4.) The Desire of Power; or the Principle of Ambition.
(5.) The Desire of Superiority; or the Principle of Emulation.

I. *The Desire of Knowledge.*

120. The principle of Curiosity appears, in children, at a very early period, and is commonly proportioned to the degree of capacity they possess. The direction too which it takes is regulated by nature, according to the order of our wants and necessities; being confined, in the first instance, exclusively to those properties of material objects, and those laws of the material world, an acquaintance with which is essential to the preservation of our animal existence. In more advanced years, it displays itself, in one way or another, in every individual; and gives rise to an infinite diversity in their pursuits. Whether this diversity be owing to natural predisposition, or to early education, it is of little consequence to determine; as upon either supposition, a preparation is made for it in the original constitution of the mind, combined with the circumstances of our external situation. Its final cause is also sufficiently obvious; as it is this which gives rise, in the case of individuals, to a limitation of attention and study; and lays the foundation of all the advantages which society derives from the division and subdivision of intellectual labour.

121. The desire of knowledge is not a selfish principle. As the object of hunger is not happiness, but food, so the object of curiosity is not happiness, but knowledge.

II. *The Desire of Society.*

122. Abstracting from those affections which interest us in the happiness of others, and from all the advantages

which we ourselves derive from the social union we are led by a natural and instinctive desire to associate with our own species. This principle is easily discernible in the minds of children, and it is common to man with many of the brutes.

123. After experiencing, indeed, the pleasures of social life; the influence of habit, and a knowledge of the comforts inseparable from society, contribute greatly to strengthen the instinctive desire: and hence some authors have been induced to display their ingenuity by disputing its existence. Whatever opinion we form on this speculative question, the desire of society is equally entitled to be ranked among the natural and universal principles of our constitution.

124. How very powerfully this principle of action operates, appears from the effects of solitude upon the mind. We feel ourselves in an unnatural state; and, by making companions of the lower animals, or by attaching ourselves to inanimate objects, strive to fill up the void of which we are conscious.

125. The connection between the Desire of Society and the Desire of Knowledge is very remarkable. The last of these principles is always accompanied with a wish to impart our information to others;—insomuch that it has been doubted if any man's curiosity would be sufficient to engage him in a course of persevering study, if he were entirely cut off from the prospect of social intercourse. In this manner, a beautiful provision is made for a mutual communication among mankind of their intellectual attainments.

III. *The Desire of Esteem.*

126. This principle discovers itself, at a very early period, in infants, who, long before they are able to reflect on the advantages resulting from the good opinion of others, and even before they acquire the use of speech, are sensibly mortified by any expression of neglect or contempt. It seems, therefore, to be an original principle of our nature; that is, it does not appear to be resolvable into reason and experience, or into any other principle more general than itself. An additional proof of this is the very powerful influence it has over the mind,—an influence more striking than that of any other active principle whatever. Even the love of life daily gives way to the desire of esteem; and of an

esteem which, as it is only to affect our memories, cannot be supposed to interest our self-love.— In what manner the association of ideas should manufacture, out of the other principles of our constitution, a new principle stronger than them all, it is difficult to conceive.

127. As our appetites of Hunger and Thirst, though not selfish principles, are yet immediately subservient to the preservation of the individual; so the desire of Esteem, though not a social or benevolent principle, is yet immediately subservient to the good of society.

IV. *The Desire of Power.*

128. Whenever we are led to consider ourselves as the authors of any effect, we feel a sensible pride or exultation in the consciousness of Power; and the pleasure is, in general, proportioned to the greatness of the effect, compared to the smallness of our exertion.

129. The infant, while still on the breast, delights in exerting its little strength upon every object it meets with, and is mortified when any accident convinces it of its own imbecility. The pastimes of the boy are, almost without exception, such as suggest to him the idea of his power:— and the same remark may be extended to the active sports and the athletic exercises of youth and of manhood.

130. As we advance in years, and as our animal powers lose their activity and vigour, we gradually aim at extending our influence over others, by the superiority of fortune and of situation, or by the still more flattering superiority of intellectual endowments:—by the force of our understanding; by the extent of our information; by the arts of persuasion, or the accomplishments of address. What but the idea of power pleases the orator, in the consciousness of his eloquence; when he silences the reason of others by superior ingenuity; bends to his purposes their desires and passions; and, without the aid of force or the splendour of rank, becomes the arbiter of the fate of nations?

131. To the same principle we may trace, in part, the pleasure arising from the discovery of general theorems. Every such discovery puts us in possession of innumerable particular truths or particular facts, and gives us a ready

command of a great stock of knowledge to which we had not access before. The desire of power, therefore, comes in the progress of reason and experience, to act as an auxiliary to our instinctive desire of knowledge.

132. The idea of power is, partly at least, the foundation of our attachment to property. It is not enough for us to have the use of an object. We desire to have it completely at our own disposal, without being responsible to any person whatever.

133. Avarice is a particular modification of the desire of power, arising from the various functions of money in a commercial country. Its influence as an active principle is much strengthened by habit and association.

134. The love of liberty proceeds, in part, from the same source, from a desire of being able to do whatever is agreeable to our own inclination. Slavery mortifies us, because it limits our power.

135. Even the love of tranquillity and retirement has been resolved by Cicero into the same principle. "Multi autem et sunt, et fuerunt, qui eam, quam dico, Tranquillitatem expetentes, a negotiis publicis se removerint, ad otiumque perfugerint. His idem propositum fuit, quod regibus; ut ne qua re egerent, ne cui parerent, libertate uterentur; cujus proprium est, sic vivere, ut velis. Quare, cum hoc commune sit potentiæ cupidorum cum iis, quos dixi, otiosis; alteri se adipisci id posse arbitrantur, si opes magnas habeant; alteri, si contenti sint et suo, et parvo."

136. The idea of power is also, in some degree, the foundation of the pleasure of Virtue. We love to be at liberty to follow our own inclinations, without being subjected to the control of a superior; but this alone is not sufficient to our happiness. When we are led by vicious habits, or by the force of passion, to do what reason disapproves, we are sensible of a mortifying subjection to the inferior principles of our nature, and feel our own littleness and weakness. A sense of freedom and independence, elevation of mind, and the pride of virtue, are the natural sentiments of the man who is conscious of being able, at all times, to calm the tumults of passion, and to obey the cool suggestions of duty and honour.

V. *The Desire of Superiority.*

137. Emulation has been sometimes classed with the Affections: but it seems more properly to fall under the definition of our Desires. It is, indeed, frequently accompanied with ill-will towards our rivals: but it is the desire of superiority which is the active principle; and the malevolent affection is only a concomitant circumstance.

138. A malevolent affection is not even a *necessary* concomitant of the desire of superiority. It is possible, surely, to conceive (although the case may happen but rarely) that Emulation may take place between men who are united by the most cordial friendship, and without a single sentiment of ill-will disturbing their harmony.

139. When Emulation is accompanied with malevolent affection, it assumes the name of Envy. The distinction between these two principles of action is accurately stated by Dr Butler. "Emulation is merely the desire of superiority over others with whom we compare ourselves. To desire the attainment of this superiority, by the particular means of others being brought down below our own level, is the distinct notion of Envy. From whence it is easy to see that the real end which the natural passion, Emulation, and which the unlawful one, Envy, aims at is exactly the same; and, consequently, that to do mischief is not the end of Envy, but merely the means it makes use of to attain its end."

140. Some faint symptoms of Emulation may be remarked among the lower animals; but the effects it produces among them are perfectly insignificant. In our own race it operates in an infinite variety of directions, and is one of the principal springs of human improvement.

141. As we have artificial appetites, so we have also artificial desires. Whatever conduces to the attainment of any object of natural desire, is itself desired on account of its subserviency to this end, and frequently comes, in process of time, to acquire, in our estimation, an intrinsic value. It is thus that wealth becomes, with many, an ultimate object of pursuit; although it is undoubtedly valued at first merely as the means of attaining other objects. In like manner men are led to desire dress, equipage, retinue,

furniture, on account of the estimation in which they are supposed to be held by the public. Such desires have been called by Dr Hutcheson, Secondary Desires. Their origin is easily explicable on the principle of Association.

SECTION IV.

Of our Affections.

142. Under this title are comprehended all those active principles whose direct and ultimate object is the communication either of enjoyment or of suffering to any of our fellow-creatures. According to this definition, Resentment, Revenge, Hatred, belong to the class of our affections, as well as Gratitude or Pity. Hence a distinction of the affections into Benevolent and Malevolent.

I. Of the Benevolent Affections.

143. Our Benevolent affections are various; and it would not, perhaps, be easy to enumerate them completely. The Parental and the Filial affections,—the affections of Kindred, —Love,—Friendship,—Patriotism,—Universal Benevolence, —Gratitude,—Pity to the distressed,—are some of the most important. Besides these, there are peculiar benevolent affections, excited by those moral qualities in other men which render them either amiable, or respectable, or objects of admiration.

144. In the foregoing enumeration it is not to be understood that all the benevolent affections particularly specified are stated as original principles, or ultimate facts in our constitution. On the contrary, there can be little doubt that several of them may be analyzed into the same general principle differently modified, according to the circumstances in which it operates. This, however, (notwithstanding the stress which has been somewhat laid upon it,) is chiefly a question of arrangement. Whether we suppose these principles to be all ultimate facts, or some of them to be resolvable into other facts more general; they are equally to be regarded as constituent parts of human nature; and upon either supposition we have equal reason to admire the

wisdom with which that nature is adapted to the situation in which it is placed.—The laws which regulate the acquired perceptions of Sight are surely as much a part of our frame as those which regulate any of our original perceptions : and although they require for their development a certain degree of experience and observation in the individual, the uniformity of the result shows that there is nothing arbitrary nor accidental in their origin.

145. The question, indeed, concerning the origin of our different affections, leads to some curious disquisitions ; but is of very subordinate importance to those inquiries which relate to their nature, and laws, and uses. In many philosophical systems, however, it seems to have been considered as the most interesting subject of discussion connected with this part of the human constitution.

146. To treat, in detail, of the nature, laws, and uses of our benevolent affections, is obviously inconsistent with the brevity of a treatise confined by its plan to a statement of definitions and divisions, and of such remarks as are necessary for explaining the arrangement on which it proceeds. The enumeration already mentioned (§ 143.) suggests an order according to which this subject may be treated in a course of lectures on Moral Philosophy. What follows is equally applicable to all the various principles which come under the general description.

147. The exercise of all our kind affections is accompanied with an agreeable feeling or emotion. So much, indeed, of our happiness is derived from this source, that those authors, whose object is to furnish amusement to the mind, avail themselves of these affections as one of the chief vehicles of pleasure. Hence, the principal charm of tragedy, and of every other species of pathetic composition. How far it is of use to separate, in this manner, " the luxury of pity " from the opportunities of active exertion, may perhaps be doubted.

148. The pleasures of kind affection are not confined to the virtuous. They mingle also with our criminal indulgences ; and often mislead the young and thoughtless, by the charms they impart, to vice and to folly.

149. Even when these affections are disappointed in the attainment of their objects, there is a degree of pleasure

mixed with the pain :—and sometimes the pleasure greatly predominates.

150. The final cause of the agreeable emotion connected with the exercise of benevolence, in all its various modes, was evidently to induce us to cultivate, with peculiar care, a class of our active principles so immediately subservient to the happiness of human society.

151. Notwithstanding, however, the pleasure arising from the indulgence of the benevolent affections, these affections have nothing selfish in their origin:—as has been fully demonstrated by different writers. This conclusion, although contrary to the systems of many philosophers, both ancient and modern, is not only agreeable to the obvious appearance of the fact, but is strongly confirmed by the analogy of the other active powers already considered.

152. We have found that the preservation of the individual, and the continuation of the species, are not intrusted to Self-love and Reason alone; but that we are endowed with various appetites, which, without any reflection on our part, impel us to their respective objects. We have also found, with respect to the acquisition of knowledge (on which the perfection of the individual and the improvement of the species essentially depend), that it is not intrusted solely to Self-love and Benevolence; but that we are prompted to it by the implanted principle of Curiosity. It further appeared that, in addition to our sense of duty, another incentive to worthy conduct is provided in the desire of Esteem, which is not only one of our most powerful principles of action, but continues to operate, in full force, to the last moment of our being. Now, as men were plainly intended to live in society, and as the social union could not subsist without a mutual interchange of good offices, would it not be reasonable to expect, agreeably to the analogy of our nature, that so important an end would not be intrusted solely to the slow deductions of Reason, or to the metaphysical refinements of Self-love; but that some provision would be made for it in a particular class of active principles, which might operate, like our appetites and desires, independently of our reflection? To say this of Parental Affection or of Pity, is saying nothing more in their favour than what was affirmed of Hunger and Thirst; that they prompt

us to particular objects, without any reference to our own enjoyment.

II. *Of the Malevolent Affections.*

153. The names which are given to these, in common discourse, are various; Hatred, Jealousy, Envy, Revenge, Misanthropy:—but it may be doubted if there be any principle of this kind implanted by nature in the mind, excepting the principle of Resentment, the others being grafted on this stock by our erroneous opinions and criminal habits.

154. Resentment has been distinguished into Instinctive and Deliberate. The former operates in man exactly as in the lower animals; and was plainly intended to guard us against sudden violence, in cases where reason would come too late to our assistance. This species of Resentment subsides as soon as we are satisfied that no injury was intended.

155. Deliberate Resentment is excited only by intentional injury; and, therefore, implies a sense of justice, or of moral good and evil.

156. The Resentment excited by an injury offered to another person is properly called Indignation. In both cases the principle of action seems to be fundamentally the same; and to have for its object, not the communication of suffering to a sensitive being, but the punishment of injustice and cruelty.

157. As all the benevolent affections are accompanied with pleasant emotions, so all the malevolent affections are sources of pain and disquiet. This is true even of Resentment; how justly soever it may be roused by the injurious conduct of others.

---

158. In the foregoing review of our active powers, no mention has been made of our Passions. The truth is, that this word does not, in strict propriety, belong exclusively to any one class of these principles; but is applicable to all of them, when they are suffered to pass the bounds of modera-

tion. In such cases, a sensible agitation or commotion of the body is produced; our reason is disturbed; we lose, in some measure, the power of self-command, and are hurried to action by an almost irresistible impulse. Ambition, the desire of Fame, Avarice, Compassion, Love, Gratitude, Resentment, Indignation, may all, in certain circumstances, be entitled to this appellation. When we speak of *passion* in general, we commonly mean the passion of Resentment; probably, because this affection disturbs the reason more, and leaves us less the power of self-government, than any other active principle of our nature.

SECTION V.

Of Self-Love.

159. The constitution of man, if it were composed merely of the active principles hitherto mentioned, would be analogous to that of the brutes. His reason, however, renders his nature and condition, on the whole, essentially different from theirs.

160. They are incapable of looking forward to consequences, or of comparing together the different gratifications of which they are susceptible; and accordingly, as far as we are able to perceive, they yield to every present impulse. But man is able to take a comprehensive survey of his various principles of action, and to form a plan of conduct for the attainment of his favourite objects. Every such plan implies a power of refusing occasionally to particular active principles the gratification which they demand.

161. According to the particular active principle which influences habitually a man's conduct, his character receives its denomination of Covetous, Ambitious, Studious, or Voluptuous; and his conduct is more or less systematical, as he adheres to his general plan with steadiness or inconstancy.

162. A systematical steadiness in the pursuit of a particular end, while it is necessary for the complete gratification of our ruling passion, is far more favourable to the general improvement of the mind than the dissipation of attention resulting from an undecided choice among the various pur-

suits which human life presents to us. Even the systematical voluptuary is able to command a much greater variety of sensual indulgences, and to continue them to a much more advanced age, than the thoughtless profligate; and, how low soever the objects may be which occupy his thoughts, they seldom fail, by engaging them habitually in one direction, to give a certain degree of cultivation to his intellectual faculties.

163. The only exception, perhaps, which can be mentioned to the last remark, is in the case of those men whose leading principle of action is *Vanity;* and who, as their rule of conduct is borrowed from without, must in consequence of this very circumstance, be perpetually wavering and inconsistent in their pursuits.—Accordingly, it will be found that such men, although they have frequently performed splendid actions, have seldom risen to eminence in any one particular career; unless when, by a rare concurrence of accidental circumstances, this career has been steadily pointed out to them through the whole of their lives by public opinion.

164. A systematical conduct in life, invariably directed to certain objects, is more favourable to happiness than one which is influenced merely by occasional inclination and appetite. Even the man who is decidedly and uniformly unprincipled, is free of much of the disquiet which disturbs the tranquillity of those whose characters are more mixed and more inconsistent.

165. There is another and very important respect in which the nature of man differs from that of the brutes. He is able to avail himself of his past experience, in avoiding those enjoyments which he knows will be succeeded by suffering; and in submitting to lesser evils which he knows are to be instrumental in procuring him a greater accession of good. He is able, in a word, to form the general notion of Happiness, and to deliberate about the most effectual means of attaining it.

166. It is implied in the very idea of happiness that it is a desirable object; and, therefore, self-love is an active principle very different from those which have been hitherto considered. These, for aught we know, may be the effect of arbitrary appointment; and they have, accordingly, been called *implanted* principles. The desire of happiness may

be called a *rational* principle of action; being peculiar to a rational nature, and inseparably connected with it.

167. In prefixing to this section the title of Self-love, the ordinary language of modern philosophy has been followed. The expression, however, is exceptionable; as it suggests an analogy (where there is none in fact) between that regard which every rational being must necessarily have to his own happiness, and those benevolent affections which attach us to our fellow-creatures.—The similarity too between the words self-love and selfishness has introduced much confusion into ethical disquisitions.

168. The word selfishness is always used in an unfavourable sense, and hence some authors have been led to suppose that vice consists in an excessive regard to our own happiness. It is remarkable, however, that although we apply the epithet *selfish* to avarice and to low and private sensuality, we never apply it to the desire of knowledge, or to the pursuits of virtue, which are certainly sources of more exquisite pleasure than riches or sensuality can bestow.

169. The truth will probably be found upon examination to be this, that the word selfishness, when applied to a pursuit, has no reference to the *motive* from which the pursuit proceeds, but to the *effect* it has on the conduct. Neither our animal appetites, nor avarice, nor curiosity, nor the desire of moral improvement, arise from self-love: but some of these active principles disconnect us with society more than others, and consequently, though they do not indicate a greater regard for our own happiness, they betray a greater unconcern for the happiness of our neighbours. The pursuits of the miser have no mixture whatever of the social affections: on the contrary, they continually lead him to state his own interest in opposition to that of other men. The enjoyments of the sensualist all expire within his own person; and therefore, whoever is habitually occupied in the search of them, must of necessity neglect the duties which he owes to mankind. It is otherwise with the desire of knowledge, which is always accompanied with a strong desire of social communication, and with the love of moral excellence, which in its practical tendency coincides so remarkably with bene-

volence, that many authors have attempted to resolve the one principle into the other.

170. That the word selfishness is by no means synonymous with a regard to our own happiness, appears further from this, that the blame we bestow on those pursuits which are commonly called selfish, is founded *partly* on the sacrifice they imply of our true interest to the inferior principles of our nature. When we see, for example, a man enslaved by his animal appetites, so far from considering him as under the influence of an excessive self-love, we pity and despise him for neglecting the higher enjoyments which are placed within his reach.

SECTION VI.

Of the Moral Faculty.

ARTICLE FIRST.

GENERAL OBSERVATIONS ON THE MORAL FACULTY; TENDING CHIEFLY TO SHOW THAT IT IS AN ORIGINAL PRINCIPLE OF OUR NATURE, AND NOT RESOLVABLE INTO ANY OTHER PRINCIPLE OR PRINCIPLES MORE SIMPLE.

171. The facts alluded to in our last paragraph of the foregoing section, have led some philosophers to conclude that Virtue is merely a matter of prudence, and that a sense of duty is but another name for a rational self-love. This view of the subject was far from being unnatural; for we find that these two principles, in general, lead to the same course of action; and we have every reason to believe that, if our knowledge of the universe were more extensive, they would be found to do so in all instances whatever.

172. That we have, however, a sense of duty, which is not resolvable into a regard to our happiness, appears from various considerations.

(1.) There are in all languages words equivalent to Duty and to Interest, which men have constantly distinguished in their signification. They coincide, in general, in their applications, but they convey very different ideas.

(2.) The emotions arising from the contemplation of what is *right* or *wrong* in conduct are different, both in degree and in kind, from those which are produced by a calm regard to our own happiness. This is particularly remarkable in the emotions excited by the moral conduct of others; for such is the influence of self-deceit, that few men judge with perfect fairness of their own actions. The emotions excited by characters exhibited in histories and in novels are sometimes still more powerful than what we experience from similar qualities displayed in the circle of our acquaintance; because the judgment is less apt to be warped by partiality or by prejudice. The representations of the stage, however, afford the most favourable of all opportunities for observing their effects. As every species of enthusiasm operates most forcibly when men are collected in a crowd, our moral feelings are exhibited on a larger scale in the theatre than in the closet. And, accordingly, the slightest hint suggested by the poet, raises to transport the passions of the audience, and forces involuntary tears from men of the greatest reserve and the most correct sense of propriety.

(3.) Although philosophers have shown that a sense of duty and an enlightened regard to our own happiness conspire, in most instances, to give the same direction to our conduct, so as to put it beyond a doubt that even in this world a virtuous life is true wisdom, yet this is a truth by no means obvious to the common sense of mankind, but deduced from an extensive view of human affairs, and an accurate investigation of the remote consequences of our different actions. It is from experience and reflection, therefore, that we learn the tendency of virtue to advance our worldly prosperity; and consequently the great lessons of morality, which are obvious to the capacity of all mankind, cannot have been suggested to them merely by a regard to their own interest.

(4.) The same conclusion is strongly confirmed by the early period of life at which our moral judgments make their appearance,—long before children are able to form the general notion of happiness, and indeed in the very infancy of their reason.

173. In order to elude the force of some of the foregoing arguments it has been supposed that the rules of morality

were, in the first instance, brought to light by the sagacity of philosophers and politicians; and that it is only in consequence of the influence of education that they appear to form an original part of the human constitution. The diversity of opinions among different nations, with respect to the morality of particular actions, has been considered as a strong confirmation of this doctrine.

174. But the power of education, although great, is confined within certain limits; for it is by co-operating with the natural principles of the mind that it produces its effects. Nay, this very susceptibility of education, which is acknowledged to belong universally to the race, pre-supposes the existence of certain principles which are common to all mankind.

175. The influence of education in diversifying the appearances which human nature exhibits, depends on that law of our constitution which was formerly called the Association of Ideas. And this law supposes in every instance that there are opinions and feelings essential to the human frame, by a combination with which external circumstances lay hold of the mind and adapt it to its accidental situation.

176. Education may vary in particular cases the opinions of individuals with respect to the beautiful and the sublime. But education could not create our notions of Beauty or Deformity, of Grandeur or Meanness. In like manner, education may vary our sentiments with respect to particular actions, but could not create our notions of Right and Wrong, of Merit and Demerit.

177. The historical facts which have been alleged to prove that the moral judgments of mankind are entirely factitious will be found upon examination to be either the effects of misrepresentation, or to lead to a conclusion directly the reverse of what has been drawn from them; proper allowance being made, 1st, For the different circumstances of mankind in different periods of society; 2ndly, For the diversity of their speculative opinions; and, 3rdly, For the different moral import of the same action, under different systems of external behaviour.

178. All these doctrines, how erroneous soever, have been maintained by writers not unfriendly to the interests of morality. But some licentious moralists have gone much

further, and have attempted to show that the motives of all men are fundamentally the same, and that what we commonly call Virtue is mere Hypocrisy.

179. The disagreeable impression which such representations of human nature leave on the mind, affords a sufficient refutation of their truth. If there be really no essential distinction between virtue and vice, whence is it that we conceive one class of qualities to be more excellent and meritorious than another? Why do we consider Pride, or Vanity, or Selfishness to be less worthy motives for our conduct than disinterested Patriotism, or Friendship, or a determined adherence to what we believe to be our duty? Why does our species appear to us less amiable in one set of philosophical systems than in another?

180. It has been a common error among licentious moralists to confound the question concerning the actual attainments of mankind with the question concerning the reality of moral distinctions, and to substitute a satire on vice and folly instead of a philosophical account of the principles of our constitution. Admitting the picture which has been sometimes drawn of the real depravity of the world to be a just one, the gloom and dissatisfaction which it leaves on the mind are sufficient to demonstrate that we are formed with the love and admiration of moral excellence, and that this is enjoined to us as the law of our nature. "Hypocrisy itself" (as Rochefoucault has remarked) "is an homage which vice renders to virtue."

SECTION VI.

Of the Moral Faculty.

ARTICLE SECOND.

ANALYSIS OF OUR MORAL PERCEPTIONS AND EMOTIONS.

181. After establishing the universality of moral perception, as an essential part of the human constitution, the next question that occurs is, how our notions of Right and Wrong are formed? Are we to refer them to a particular principle in our nature, appropriated to the perception of these qualities, as our external senses are appropriated to the percep-

tion of the qualities of matter?—or are they perceived by the same intellectual power which discovers truth in the abstract sciences?—or are they resolvable into other notions still more simple and general than themselves? All these opinions have been maintained by authors of eminence. In order to form a judgment on the point in dispute it is necessary to analyze the state of our minds when we are spectators of any good or bad action performed by another person, or when we reflect on the actions performed by ourselves. On such occasions we are conscious of three different things.

(1.) The perception of an action as Right or Wrong.

(2.) An emotion of pleasure or of pain, varying in its degree, according to the acuteness of our moral sensibility.

(3.) A perception of the merit or demerit of the agent.

I. *Of the Perception of Right and Wrong.*

182. The controversy concerning the origin of our moral ideas took its rise in modern times, in consequence of the writings of Mr Hobbes. According to him we approve of virtuous actions, or of actions beneficial to society, from self-love; as we know that whatever promotes the interest of society has, on that very account, an indirect tendency to promote our own.—He further taught that, as it is to the institution of government we are indebted for all the comforts and the confidence of social life, the laws which the civil magistrate enjoins are the ultimate standards of morality.

183. Dr Cudworth, who, in opposition to the system of Mr Hobbes, first showed in a satisfactory manner that our ideas of Right and Wrong are not derived from positive law, referred the origin of these ideas to the power which distinguishes truth from falsehood; and it became for some time the fashionable language among moralists to say that virtue consisted, not in obedience to the law of a superior, but in a conduct conformable to Reason.

184. At the time that Cudworth wrote no accurate classification had been attempted of the principles of the human mind. His account of the office of reason, accordingly, in enabling us to perceive the distinction between right and wrong, passed without censure, and was understood merely to imply

that there is an eternal and immutable distinction between right and wrong, no less than between truth and falsehood; and that both these distinctions are perceived by our rational powers, or by those powers which raise us above the brutes.

185. The publication of Locke's Essay introduced into this part of science a precision of expression unknown before, and taught philosophers to distinguish a variety of powers which had formerly been very generally confounded. With these great merits, however, his work has capital defects; and, perhaps, in no part of it are these defects more important than in the attempt he has made to deduce the origin of our knowledge entirely from sensation and reflection. These, according to him, are the sources of all our simple ideas; and the only power that the mind possesses is to perform certain operations of Analysis, Combination, Comparison, &c., on the materials with which it is thus supplied.

186. This system led Mr Locke to some dangerous opinions concerning the nature of moral distinctions, which he seems to have considered as the offspring of Education and Fashion. Indeed, if the words Right and Wrong neither express simple ideas, nor relations discoverable by reason, it will not be found easy to avoid adopting this conclusion.

187. In order to reconcile Locke's account of the origin of our ideas with the immutability of moral distinctions, different theories were proposed concerning the nature of virtue. According to one, for example, it was said to consist in a conduct conformable to the fitness of things: according to another, in a conduct conformable to Truth.—The great object of all these theories may be considered as the same,— to remove Right and Wrong from the class of simple ideas, and to resolve moral rectitude into a conformity with some relation perceived by reason or the understanding.

188. Dr Hutcheson saw clearly the vanity of these attempts; and hence he was led, in compliance with the language of Locke's philosophy, to refer the origin of our moral ideas to a particular power of perception, to which he gave the name of the Moral Sense. "All the ideas (says he), or the materials of our reasoning or judging, are received by some immediate powers of perception, internal or external, which we may call senses. Reasoning or intellect seems to

raise no new species of ideas, but to discover or discern the relations of those received."

189. According to this system, as it has been commonly explained, our perceptions of right and wrong are impressions which our minds are made to receive from particular actions; similar to the relishes and aversions given us for particular objects of the external or internal senses.

190. From the hypothesis of a moral sense various sceptical conclusions have been deduced by later writers. The words Right and Wrong, it has been alleged, signify nothing in the objects themselves to which they are applied, any more than the words sweet and bitter, pleasant and painful; but only certain effects in the mind of the spectator. As it is improper, therefore (according to the doctrines of modern philosophy), to say of an object of taste, that it is sweet; or of heat, that it is in the fire; so it is equally improper to say of actions, that they are right or wrong. It is absurd to speak of morality as a thing independent and unchangeable; inasmuch as it arises from an arbitrary relation between our constitution and particular objects.

191. In order to avoid these supposed consequences of Dr Hutcheson's philosophy, an attempt has been made by some later writers, in particular by Dr Price, to revive the doctrines of Dr Cudworth, and to prove that moral distinctions, being perceived by reason or the understanding, are equally immutable with all other kinds of truth.

192. This is the most important question that can be stated with respect to the theory of morals. The obscurity in which it is involved arises chiefly from the use of indefinite and ambiguous terms.

193. That moral distinctions are perceived by a sense, is implied in the definition of a sense which Dr Hutcheson has given (§ 188): provided it be granted (as Dr Price has done explicitly) that the words Right and Wrong express simple ideas, or ideas incapable of analysis.

194. It may be further observed, in justification of Dr Hutcheson, that the sceptical consequences deduced from his supposition of a moral sense do not necessarily result from it. Unfortunately, most of his illustrations were taken from the secondary qualities of matter, which, since the time of Des Cartes, philosophers have been in general accustomed

to refer to the mind, and not to the external object. But if we suppose our perception of Right and Wrong to be analogous to the perception of Extension and Figure and other primary qualities, the reality and immutability of moral distinctions seems to be placed on a foundation sufficiently satisfactory to a candid inquirer (§ 31 and 32).

195. The definition, however, of a sense, which Hutcheson has given, is by far too general, and was plainly suggested to him by Locke's account of the origin of our ideas (§ 185). The words Cause and Effect, Duration, Number, Equality, Identity, and many others, express simple ideas, as well as the words Right and Wrong; and yet it would surely be absurd to ascribe each of them to a particular power of perception. Notwithstanding this circumstance, as the expression *Moral Sense* has now the sanction of use, and as, when properly explained, it cannot lead to any bad consequences, it may be still retained, without inconvenience, in ethical disquisitions.

196. To what part of our constitution, then, shall we ascribe the origin of the ideas of Right and Wrong? Price says,—to the Understanding; and endeavours to show, in opposition to Locke and his followers, that "the power which understands, or the faculty that discerns truth, is a source of new ideas."

197. This controversy turns chiefly on the meaning of words. The origin of our ideas of right and wrong is manifestly the same with that of the other simple ideas already mentioned; and, whether it be referred to the understanding or not, seems to be a matter of mere arrangement; provided it be granted that the words Right and Wrong express qualities of actions, and not merely a power of exciting certain agreeable or disagreeable emotions in our minds.

198. It may perhaps obviate some objections against the language of Cudworth and Price to remark, that the word Reason is used in senses which are extremely different. Sometimes to express the whole of those powers which elevate man above the brutes, and constitute his rational nature; more especially, perhaps, his intellectual powers. Sometimes to express the power of deduction or argumentation. The former is the sense in which the word is used in common discourse; and it is in this sense that it seems

to be employed by those writers who refer to it the origin of our moral ideas. Their antagonists, on the other hand, understand in general by Reason, the power of deduction or argumentation, a use of the word which is not unnatural, from the similarity between the words Reason and Reasoning, but which is not agreeable to its ordinary meaning. "No hypothesis (say Dr Campbell) hitherto invented hath shown that, by means of the discursive faculty, without the aid of any other mental power, we could ever obtain a notion of either the beautiful or the good."[1] The remark is undoubtedly true, and may be applied to all those systems which ascribe to Reason the origin of our moral ideas, if the expressions Reason and Discursive Faculty be used as synonymous. But if the word Reason be used in a more general sense to denote merely our rational and intellectual nature, there does not seem to be much impropriety in ascribing to it the origin of those simple notions which are not excited in the mind by the immediate operation of the senses; but which arise in consequence of the exercise of the intellectual powers upon their various objects.

199. A variety of intuitive judgments might be mentioned, involving simple ideas, which it is impossible to trace to any origin but to the power which enables us to form these judgments. Thus it is surely an intuitive truth, that the sensations of which I am conscious, and all those I remember, belong to one and the same being, which I call *myself*. Here is an intuitive judgment involving the simple idea of *Identity*.—In like manner, the changes which I perceive in the universe impress me with a conviction that some cause must have operated to produce them. Here is an intuitive judgment, involving the simple idea of *Causation*.—When we consider the adjacent angles made by a straight line standing upon another, and perceive that their sum is equal to two right angles, the judgment we form involves the simple idea of *Equality*.—To say, therefore, that Reason or the Understanding is a source of new ideas, is not so exceptionable a mode of speaking as has been sometimes supposed.—According to Locke, *Sense* furnishes our ideas, and *Reason* perceives their agreements or disagreements. But

[1] Philosophy of Rhetoric, vol. i. page 204.

the truth is that these agreements and disagreements are, in many instances, simple ideas, of which no analysis can be given; and of which the origin must therefore be referred to Reason, according to Locke's own doctrine.

200. The opinion we form, however, on this point is of little moment, provided it be granted that the words Right and Wrong express qualities of actions. When I say of an act of justice that it is right, do I mean merely that the act excites pleasure in my mind, as a particular colour pleases my eye in consequence of a relation which it bears to my organ; or do I mean to assert a truth which is as independent of my constitution as the equality of the three angles of a triangle to two right angles? Scepticism may be indulged in both cases about mathematical and about moral truth; but in neither case does it admit of a refutation by argument.

201. The immutability of moral distinctions has been called in question, not only by sceptical writers, but by some philosophers who have adopted their doctrine, with the pious design of magnifying the perfections of the Deity. Such authors certainly do not recollect that what they add to his power and majesty they take away from his moral attributes; for if moral distinctions be not immutable and eternal, it is absurd to speak of the goodness or of the justice of God.

II. *Of the Agreeable and Disagreeable Emotions arising from the Perception of what is Right and Wrong in Conduct.*

202. It is impossible to behold a good action without being conscious of a benevolent affection, either of love or of respect, towards the agent; and consequently, as all our benevolent affections include an agreeable feeling, every good action must be a source of pleasure to the spectator. Beside this, other agreeable feelings of order, of utility, of peace of mind, &c., come in process of time to be associated with the general idea of virtuous conduct.

203. Those qualities in good actions which excite agreeable feelings in the mind of the spectator, form what some moralists have called the Beauty of Virtue.

204. All this may be applied, *mutatis mutandis*, to explain what is meant by the Deformity of Vice.

205. Our perception of moral beauty and deformity is plainly distinguishable from our perception of actions as right or wrong. But the distinction has been too little attended to by philosophers.—Among the moderns in particular, some have confined their attention almost solely to our perception of actions as right or wrong, and have thereby rendered their works abstract and uninteresting. Others, by dwelling exclusively on our perception of Moral Beauty and Deformity, have been led into enthusiasm and declamation, and have furnished licentious moralists with a pretext for questioning the immutability of moral distinctions.

206. The emotions of pleasure and of pain arising from the contemplation of moral beauty and deformity, are so much more exquisite than any that are produced by the perception of material forms, that some philosophers have held that the words Beauty and Sublimity express, in their *literal* signification, the qualities of mind; and that material objects affect us only by means of the moral ideas they suggest. This was a favourite doctrine of the Socratic school, and has been supported with great ingenuity by several modern writers.

207. Whatever opinion we adopt on this speculative question, there can be no dispute about the fact, that good actions and virtuous characters form the most delightful of all objects to the human mind; and that there are no charms in the external universe so powerful as those which recommend to us the cultivation of the qualities that constitute the perfection and happiness of our nature.

208. It was a leading object of the ancient moralists, to establish such a union between philosophy and the fine arts, as might add to the natural beauty of virtue every attraction which the imagination could impart to her. The effect which might be produced in this way may be easily conceived, from the examples we daily see of the influence of association in concealing the meanness and deformity of fashionable vices.

III. *Of the Perception of Merit and Demerit.*

209. The virtuous actions performed by other men, not only excite in our minds a benevolent affection towards them, or a disposition to promote their happiness, but impress us with a sense of the merit of the agents. We perceive them to be the proper objects of love and esteem, and that it is morally right that they should receive their reward. We feel ourselves called on to make their worth known to the world in order to procure them the favour and respect they deserve, and if we allow it to remain secret we are conscious of injustice in suppressing the natural language of the heart.

210. On the other hand, when we are witnesses of an act of selfishness, of cruelty, or of oppression; whether we ourselves are the sufferers or not, we are not only inspired with aversion and hatred towards the delinquent, but find it difficult to restrain our indignation from breaking loose against him. By this natural impulse of the mind a check is imposed on the bad passions of individuals; and a provision is made, even before the establishment of positive laws, for the good order of society.

211. In our own case, when we are conscious of doing well we feel that we are entitled to the esteem and attachment of our fellow-creatures; and we know, with the evidence of a perception, that we enjoy the approbation of the invisible witness of our conduct. Hence it is that we have not only a sense of merit, but an anticipation of reward, and look forwards to the future with increased confidence and hope.

212. The feelings of remorse which accompany the consciousness of guilt involve, in like manner, a sense of ill-desert, and an anticipation of future punishment.

213. Although, however, our sense of Merit and Demerit must convince the philosopher of the connection which the Deity has established between virtue and happiness, he does not proceed on the supposition, that on particular occasions miraculous interpositions are to be made in his favour. That virtue is, even in this world, the most direct road to happiness he sees to be a fact, but he knows that the Deity governs by general laws, and when he feels himself disap-

pointed in the attainment of his wishes he acquiesces in his lot, and consoles himself with the prospect of futurity. It is an error of the vulgar to expect that good or bad fortune are always to be connected, in particular instances, with good or bad actions,—a prejudice which is a source of much disappointment in human life, but of which the prevalence in all ages and countries affords a striking illustration of the natural connection between the ideas of virtue and of merit.

SECTION VI.

Of the Moral Faculty.

ARTICLE THIRD.

OF MORAL OBLIGATION.

214. According to some systems, moral obligation is founded entirely on our belief that virtue is enjoined by the command of God. But how, it may be asked, does this belief impose an obligation? Only one of two answers can be given. Either that there is a moral fitness that we should conform our will to that of the Author and the Governor of the universe; or that a rational self-love should induce us, out of prudence, to study every means of rendering ourselves acceptable to the almighty Arbiter of happiness and misery. On the first supposition we reason in a circle. We resolve our sense of moral obligation into our sense of religion; and the sense of religion into that of moral obligation.

215. The other system, which makes virtue a mere matter of prudence, although not so obviously unsatisfactory, leads to consequences which sufficiently show that it is erroneous. Among others it leads us to conclude, 1. That the disbelief of a future state absolves from all moral obligation, excepting in so far as we find virtue to be conducive to our present interest;—2. That a being independently and completely happy cannot have any moral perceptions, or any moral attributes.

216. But further, the notions of reward and punishment presuppose the notions of right and wrong. They are sanctions of virtue, or additional motives to the practice of it;

but they suppose the existence of some previous obligation.

217. In the last place, if moral obligation be constituted by a regard to our situation in another life, how shall the existence of a future state be proved by the light of nature ? or how shall we discover what conduct is acceptable to the Deity ? The truth is, that the strongest argument for such a state is deduced from our natural notions of right and wrong, of merit and demerit; and from a comparison between these and the general course of human affairs.

218. It is absurd therefore to ask, why we are bound to practise virtue ? The very notion of virtue implies the notion of obligation. Every being who is conscious of the distinction between Right and Wrong, carries about with him a law which he is bound to observe; notwithstanding he may be in total ignorance of a future state. " What renders obnoxious to punishment is not the foreknowledge of it, but merely the violating a known obligation."*

219. From what has been stated, it follows that the moral faculty, considered as an active power of the mind, differs essentially from all the others hitherto enumerated. The least violation of its authority fills us with remorse. On the contrary, the greater the sacrifices we make, in obedience to its suggestions, the greater are our satisfaction and triumph.

220. The supreme authority of conscience, although beautifully described by many of the ancient moralists, was not sufficiently attended to by modern writers as a fundamental principle in the science of ethics till the time of Dr Butler. Too little stress is laid on it by Lord Shaftesbury; and the omission is the chief defect of his philosophy.

221. If this distinction between the moral faculty and our other active powers be acknowledged, it is of the less consequence what particular theory we adopt concerning the origin of our moral ideas : and accordingly Mr Smith, though he resolves moral approbation ultimately into a feeling of the mind, represents the supremacy of conscience as a principle which is equally essential to all the different systems that have been proposed on the subject. " Upon whatever

* Butler.

we suppose our moral faculties to be founded, whether upon a certain modification of reason, upon an original instinct, called a moral sense, or upon some other principle of our nature, it cannot be doubted that they were given us for the direction of our conduct in this life. They carry along with them the most evident badges of this authority, which denote that they were set up within us to be the supreme arbiters of all our actions, to superintend all our senses, passions, and appetites, and to judge how far each of them was either to be indulged or restrained.—It is the peculiar office of these faculties to judge, to bestow censure or applause upon all the other principles of our nature."

SECTION VII.

Of certain Principles which co-operate with our Moral Powers in their Influence on the Conduct.

222. In order to secure still more completely the good order of society, and to facilitate the acquisition of virtuous habits, nature has superadded to our moral constitution a variety of auxiliary principles, which sometimes give rise to a conduct agreeable to the rules of morality, and highly useful to mankind; where the merit of the individual considered as a moral agent is extremely inconsiderable. Hence some of them have been confounded with our moral powers, or even supposed to be of themselves sufficient to account for the phenomena of moral perception, by authors whose views of human nature have not been sufficiently comprehensive.—The most important principles of this description are, 1. A regard to Character. 2. Sympathy. 3. The sense of the Ridiculous. And. 4. Taste.—The principle of Self-love (which was treated of in a former section) co-operates powerfully to the same purposes.

I. *Of Decency, or a regard to Character.*

223. It was before observed (§ 126) that the desire of esteem operates in children before they have a capacity of distinguishing right from wrong; and that the former principle of action continues for a long time to be much more powerful than the latter. Hence it furnishes a most useful

and effectual engine in the business of education; more particularly by training us early to exertions of self-command and self-denial. It teaches us, for example, to restrain our appetites within those bounds which *decency* prescribes, and thus forms us to habits of moderation and temperance. And, although our conduct cannot be denominated virtuous so long as a regard to the opinion of others is our only motive, yet the habits we thus acquire in infancy and childhood render it more easy for us, as we advance to maturity, to subject our passions to the authority of reason and conscience.

224. That our sense of duty is not resolvable into a desire of obtaining the good opinion of our fellow-creatures may be inferred from the following considerations.

1. The desire of esteem can only be effectually gratified by the actual possession of those qualities for which we wish to be esteemed.

2. The merit of a virtuous action is always enhanced in the opinion of mankind, when it is discovered in those situations of life where the individual cannot be suspected of any view to the applauses of the world.

3. When a competition takes place between our sense of duty and a regard to public opinion; if we sacrifice the former to the latter we are filled with remorse and self-condemnation, and the applause of the multitude afford us but an empty and unsatisfactory recompense; whereas a steady adherence to the Right never fails to be its own reward, even when it exposes us to calumny and misrepresentation.

II. *Of Sympathy.*

225. That there is an exquisite pleasure annexed to the sympathy or fellow-feeling of other men, with our joys and sorrows, and even with our opinions, tastes, and humours, is a fact obvious to vulgar observation. It is no less evident that we feel a disposition to accommodate the state of our own minds to that of our companions, wherever we feel a benevolent affection towards them; and that this accommodating temper is in proportion to the strength of our affection. In such cases, sympathy would appear to be grafted on benevolence; and perhaps it might be found, on

an accurate analysis, that the greater part of the pleasures which it yields is resolvable into those which arise from the exercise of kindness and from the consciousness of being beloved.

226. The same word, *sympathy*, is applied in a loose and popular sense to various phenomena in the Animal Economy; to the correspondence, for example, in the motions of the eyes, and to the connection which exists between different organs of the body, in respect of health or of disease. It is also applied to those contagious bodily affections which one person is apt to catch from another; such as yawning, stammering, squinting, sore eyes, and the disorders commonly distinguished by the name of Hysterical.

227. In all these different instances there is, no doubt, a certain degree of analogy; such as completely accounts for their being comprehended, in ordinary discourse, under one general name; but, where philosophical precision is aimed at, there is ground for many distinctions. Hence the necessity of limiting, by an accurate definition, the sense in which this very vague and equivocal word is to be understood when it is introduced into any scientific discussion.

228. The facts generally referred to *sympathy* have appeared to Mr Smith so important and so curiously connected that he has been led to attempt an explanation, from this single principle, of all the phenomena of moral perception.

229. The large mixture of valuable truth contained in this most ingenious Theory, and the light which it throws on a part of our frame, formerly very little attended to by Philosophers, entitles the Author to the highest rank among Systematical Moralists; but on a closer examination of the subject, it will be found that he has been misled like many other eminent writers by an excessive love of simplicity; mistaking a subordinate principle in our moral constitution (or rather a principle *superadded* to our moral constitution, as an auxiliary to the sense of duty) for that Faculty which distinguishes Right from Wrong; and which (by what name soever we may choose to distinguish it) recurs on us constantly in all our ethical disquisitions, as an ultimate fact in the nature of man.

III. *Of the Sense of the Ridiculous.*

230. The natural and proper object of Ridicule, is those smaller improprieties in character and manners which do not rouse our feelings of moral indignation, nor impress us with a melancholy view of human depravity.

231. While this part of our constitution enlarges the fund of our enjoyment, by rendering the more trifling imperfections of our fellow-creatures a source of amusement to their neighbours, it excites the exertions of every individual to correct those imperfections by which the ridicule of others is likely to be provoked. As our eagerness, too, to correct these imperfections may be presumed to be weak in proportion as we apprehend them to be, in a moral view, of trifling moment, we are so formed that the painful feelings produced by ridicule are often more poignant than those arising from the consciousness of having rendered ourselves the objects of resentment or of hatred.

232. The sense of the Ridiculous, although it has a manifest reference to such a scene of imperfection as we are placed in at present, is one of the most striking characteristics of the human constitution, as distinguished from that of the lower animals; and has an intimate connection with its highest and noblest principles. In the education of youth nothing requires more serious attention than its proper regulation.

IV. *Of Taste, considered in its relation to Morals.*

233. From the explanation formerly given (202, 203, 204) of the import of the phrases *Moral Beauty* and *Moral Deformity*, it may be easily conceived in what manner the character and the conduct of our fellow-creatures may become subservient to the gratification of Taste. The use which the Poet makes of this class of our intellectual pleasures is entirely analogous to the resources which he borrows from the charms of external nature.

234. The power of moral taste, like that which has for its object the beauty of material forms and the various productions of the fine arts, requires much exercise for its development and culture. The one species of taste also, as

well as the other, is susceptible of a false refinement, injurious to our own happiness, and to our usefulness as members of society.

235. Considered as a principle of action, a cultivated moral taste, while it provides an effectual security against the grossness necessarily connected with many vices, cherishes a temper of mind friendly to all that is amiable or generous or elevated in our nature. When separated, however, as it sometimes is, from a strong sense of duty, it can scarcely fail to prove a fallacious guide; the influence of fashion, and of other casual associations, tending perpetually to lead it astray. This is more particularly remarkable in men to whom the gratifications of *Taste in general* form the principal object of pursuit; and whose habits of life encourage them to look no higher for their rule of judgment than the way of the world.

236. The language employed by some of the Greek Philosophers in their speculations concerning the nature of virtue, seems, on a superficial view, to imply that they supposed the moral faculty to be wholly resolvable into a sense of the Beautiful. And hence Lord Shaftesbury and others have been led to adopt a phraseology which has the appearance of substituting Taste in contradistinction to Reason and Conscience, as the ultimate standard of Right and Wrong.

---

237. From each of the four principles now enumerated unfortunate consequences result, wherever it prevails in the character as the leading motive to action. Where they all maintain their due place in subordination to the moral faculty, they tend, at once, to fortify virtuous habits, and to recommend them by the influence of amiable example to the imitation of others.

238. A partial consideration of the phenomena of moral perception, connected with one or other of these principles, has suggested some of the most popular theories concerning the origin of our moral ideas. An attention to the moral faculty alone, without regard to the principles which were intended to operate as its auxiliaries, and which contribute, in fact, so powerfully to the good order of society, has led a few philosophers into an opposite extreme; less dangerous,

undoubtedly, in its practical tendency, but less calculated perhaps to recommend ethical disquisitions to the notice of those who are engrossed with the active concerns of life.

SECTION VIII.

Of Man's Free Agency.

239. All the foregoing inquiries concerning the moral constitution of man proceed on the supposition that he has a freedom of choice between good and evil; and that when he deliberately performs an action which he knows to be wrong, he renders himself justly obnoxious to punishment. That this supposition is agreeable to the common apprehensions of mankind will not be disputed.

240. From very early ages, indeed, the truth of the supposition has been called in question by a few speculative men, who have contended that the actions we perform are the necessary result of the constitutions of our minds operated on by the circumstances of our external situation; and that what we commonly call moral delinquencies are as much a part of our destiny as the corporeal or intellectual qualities we have received from nature.—The argument in support of this doctrine has been proposed in various forms, and has been frequently urged with the confidence of demonstration.

241. Among those, however, who hold the language of Necessitarians, an important distinction must be made, as some of them not only admit the reality of moral distinctions, but insist that it is on their hypothesis alone that these distinctions are conceivable. With such men the scheme of necessity may be a harmless opinion; and there is ground even for suspecting that it might be found to differ from that of their antagonists, more in appearance than in reality, if due pains were taken to fix the meaning of the indefinite and ambiguous terms which have been employed on both sides of the argument.

242. By other philosophers the consequences which are generally supposed to be connected with this system have been admitted in all their extent; or rather, the system has been inculcated with a view to establish these consequences.

When proposed in this form it furnishes the most interesting subject of discussion which can employ human ingenuity, and upon which our speculative opinions can hardly fail to affect very materially both our conduct and our happiness.

243. Dr Cudworth, who wrote towards the end of the seventeenth century, observes that "the scepticism which flourished in his time grew up from the doctrine of the fatal necessity of all actions and events, as from its proper root." The same remark will be found to apply to the sceptical philosophy of the present age.

244. It is sufficient in these Outlines to mark the place which the question seems naturally to occupy in the order of study. Detached hints would throw but little additional light on a controversy which has been industriously darkened by all the powers of sophistry.

PART II.

OF THE ACTIVE AND OF THE MORAL POWERS OF MAN.

CHAPTER II.

OF THE VARIOUS BRANCHES OF OUR DUTY.

245. THE different theories which have been proposed concerning the nature and essence of Virtue, have arisen chiefly from attempts to trace all the branches of our duty to one principle of action; such as a rational Self-love, Benevolence, Justice, or a disposition to obey the will of God.

246. In order to avoid those partial views of the subject which naturally take their rise from an undue love of system, the following inquiries proceed upon an arrangement which has in all ages recommended itself to the good sense of mankind. This arrangement is founded on the different objects to which our duties relate. 1. The Deity. 2. Our Fellow-creatures. And, 3. Ourselves.

SECTION I.

Of the Duties which respect the Deity.

247. As our duties to God (so far as they are discoverable by the light of nature) must be inferred from the relation in which we stand to him as the Author and the Governor of the Universe, an examination of the principles of Natural Religion forms a necessary introduction to this section. Such an examination, besides being the reasonable consequence of those impressions which his works produce on every attentive and well-disposed mind, may be itself regarded both as one of the duties we owe to Him, and as the expression of a moral temper sincerely devoted to truth, and alive to the sublimest emotions of gratitude and of benevolence.

PRELIMINARY INQUIRY INTO THE PRINCIPLES OF NATURAL RELIGION.

ARTICLE FIRST.
OF THE EXISTENCE OF THE DEITY.

248. On this subject two modes of reasoning have been employed, which are commonly distinguished by the titles of the Arguments *à priori* and *à posteriori;* the former, founded on certain metaphysical propositions which are assumed as axioms; the latter appealing to that systematical order and those combinations of means to ends which are everywhere conspicuous in Nature.

249. The argument *à priori* has been enforced with singular ingenuity by Dr Clarke, whose particular manner of stating it seems to have been suggested to him by the following passage in Newton's Principia: "Æternus est et infinitus, omnipotens et omnisciens; id est, durat ab æterno in æternum, et adest ab infinito in infinitum.—Non est æternitas et infinitas, sed æternus et infinitus; non est duratio et spatium, sed durat et adest. Durat semper, et adest ubique; et existendo semper et ubique, durationem et

spatium constituit." * Proceeding on the same principles, Dr Clarke argues that "space and time are only abstract conceptions of an immensity and eternity which force themselves on our belief; and, as immensity and eternity are not substances, they must be the attributes of a being who is necessarily immense and eternal."—"These (says Dr Reid) are the speculations of men of superior genius; but whether they be as solid as they are sublime, or whether they be the wanderings of imagination in a region beyond the limits of human understanding, I am unable to determine."

250. Without calling in question the solidity of Clarke's demonstration, we may be allowed to say that the argument *à posteriori* is more level to the comprehension of ordinary men, and more satisfactory to the philosopher himself. Indeed, in inquiries of this sort, the presumption is strongly in favour of that mode of reasoning which is the most simple and obvious.—" Quicquid nos vel meliores vel beatiores facturum est, aut in aperto, aut in proximo, posuit natura."

251. The existence of a Deity, however, does not seem to be an intuitive truth. It requires the exercise of our reasoning powers to present it in its full force to the mind. But the process of reasoning consists only of a single step; and the premises belong to that class of first principles which form an essential part of the human constitution, (§ 71 (3). These premises are two in number. The one is, that everything which begins to exist must have a cause. The other, that a combination of means conspiring to a particular end implies intelligence.

I. *Of the Foundations of our Reasoning from the Effect to the Cause, and of the Evidences of Active Power exhibited in the Universe.*

252. It was before observed (Introd. § 3) that our knowledge of the course of nature is entirely the result of observation and experiment; and that there is no instance in which we perceive such a connection between two successive events, as might enable us to infer the one from the other as a necessary consequence.

* Newton. Princ. Scholium generale.

253. From this principle, which is now very generally admitted by philosophers, Mr Hume has deduced an objection to the argument *à posteriori* for the existence of the Deity. After having proved that we cannot get the idea of necessary connection from examining the conjunction between any two events, he takes for granted that we have no other idea of Cause and Effect than of two successive events which are invariably conjoined; that we have therefore no reason to think that any one event in nature is necessarily connected with another, or to infer the operation of power from the changes which we observe in the universe.

254. To perceive the connection between Mr Hume's premises and his conclusion, it is necessary to recollect that, according to his system, "all our ideas are nothing but copies of our impressions; or, in other words, that it is impossible for us to *think* of anything which we have not antecedently *felt*, either by our external or internal senses." Having proved, therefore, that external objects, as they appear to our senses, give us no idea of power or of necessary connection, and also that this idea cannot be copied from any internal impression (that is, cannot be derived from reflection on the operations of our own minds), he thinks himself warranted to conclude that we have no such idea. "One event (says he) follows another, but we never observe any tie between them. They seem *conjoined* but never *connected*. And as we can have no idea of anything which never appeared to our outward sense or inward sentiment, the necessary conclusion seems to be, That we have no idea of connection or power at all; and that these words are absolutely without any meaning when employed either in philosophical reasonings or common life."

255. Are we, therefore, to reject as perfectly unintelligible a word which is to be found in all languages, merely because it expresses an idea, for the origin of which we cannot account upon a particular philosophical system? Would it not be more reasonable to suspect that the system was not perfectly complete, than that all mankind should have agreed in employing a word which conveyed no meaning?

256. With respect to Mr Hume's theory concerning the origin of our ideas, it is the less necessary to enter into particular discussions, that it coincides, in the main, with the

doctrine of Locke, to which some objections, which appear to be insurmountable, were formerly stated (§ 199). Upon neither theory is it possible to explain the origin of those simple notions which are not received immediately by any external sense, nor derived immediately from our own consciousness; but which are necessarily formed by the mind, while we are exercising our intellectual powers upon their proper objects.

257. These very slight hints are sufficient to show that we are not entitled to dispute the reality of our idea of power because we cannot trace it to any of our senses. The only question is, If it be certain that we annex any idea to the word power different from that of mere succession? The following considerations, among many others, prove that the import of these two expressions is by no means the same.

(1.) If we had no idea of cause and effect different from that of mere succession, it would appear to us no less absurd to suppose two events disjoined which we have constantly seen connected, than to suppose a change to take place without a cause. The former supposition, however, is easy in all cases whatever. The latter may be safely pronounced to be impossible.

(2.) Our experience of the established connections of physical events is by far too narrow a foundation for our belief that every change must have a cause. Mr Hume himself has observed that "the vulgar always include the idea of *Contiguity in place* in the idea of causation;" or, in other words, that they conceive matter to produce its effects by impulse alone. If, therefore, every change which had fallen under our notice had been preceded by apparent impulse, experience might have taught us to conclude, from observing a change, that a previous impulse had been given; or, according to Mr Hume's notion of *a cause*, that a cause had operated to produce this effect. Of the changes, however, which we see, how small a number is produced by apparent impulse! And yet, in the case of every change, without exception, we have an irresistible conviction of the operation of some cause. How shall we explain, on Mr Hume's principles, the foundation of this conviction in cases in which impulse has apparently no share?

258. The question, however, still recurs, In what manner do we acquire the idea of Causation, Power, or Efficiency? —But this question, if the foregoing observations be admit-

ted, is comparatively of little consequence, as the doubts which may arise on the subject tend only (without affecting the reality of the idea or notion) to expose the defects of particular philosophical systems.

259. The most probable account of the matter seems to be that the idea of causation or of power necessarily accompanies the perception of change, in a way somewhat analogous to that in which sensation implies a being who feels, and thought, a being who thinks. A power of beginning motion, for example, is an attribute of mind, no less than sensation or thought, and wherever motion commences we have evidence that mind has operated.

260. Are we therefore to conclude that the divine power is constantly exerted to produce the phenomena of the material world, and to suppose that one and the same cause produces that infinite multiplicity of effects which are every moment taking place in the universe?

261. In order to avoid this conclusion, which has been thought by many too absurd to deserve a serious examination, various hypotheses have been proposed. The most important of these may be referred to the following heads.

(1.) That the phenomena of nature are the result of certain active powers essentially inherent in matter. This doctrine is commonly called *Materialism*.

(2.) That they result from certain active powers communicated to matter at its first formation.

(3.) That they take place in consequence of general laws established by the Deity.

(4.) That they are produced by " a vital and spiritual but unintelligent and necessary agent, created by the Deity for the execution of his purposes." *

(5.) That they are produced by *minds* connected with the particles of matter.

(6.) That the universe is a machine formed and put in motion by the Deity; and that the multiplicity of effects which take place may perhaps have all proceeded from one single act of his power.

262. These different hypotheses (some of them which will be found, on examination, to resolve into unmeaning or un-

* Cudworth.

intelligible propositions, and all of which are liable to insurmountable objections) have been adopted by ingenious men, in preference to the simple and sublime doctrine which supposes the order of the universe to be not only at first established, but every moment maintained, by the incessant agency of One Supreme Mind;—a doctrine, against which no objection can be stated but what is founded on prejudices resulting from our own imperfections.—This doctrine does not exclude the possibility of the Deity's acting occasionally by subordinate agents or instruments.

263. The observations, indeed, hitherto made are not sufficient of themselves to authorize us to form any conclusion with respect to the unity of God, but when properly illustrated they will be found to warrant fully the following inference: That the phenomena of the universe indicate the constant agency of powers which cannot belong to matter; or, in other words, that they indicate the constant agency of Mind. Whether these phenomena, when compared together, bear marks of a diversity of a unity of design; and, of consequence, whether they suggest the Government of one almighty Ruler, or of a plurality of independent divinities, are inquiries which belong to the next head of our argument.

II. *Of the Evidences of Design exhibited in the Universe.*

264. The proof of the existence of God, drawn from the Order of the universe, is commonly called the argument from Final Causes. The expression (which was first introduced by Aristotle) is far from being proper, but is retained in this treatise in compliance with established use.

265. It is justly remarked by Dr Reid that the argument from Final Causes, when reduced to a syllogism, contains two propositions. The major is, That Design may be traced from its effects. The minor, That there are appearances of Design in the universe. The ancient sceptics, he says, granted the first, but denied the second. The moderns (in consequence of the discoveries in natural philosophy) have been obliged to abandon the ground which their predecessors maintained, and have disputed the major proposition.

266. Among those who have denied the possibility of tracing design from its effects, Mr Hume is the most emi-

nent. According to him, all such inferences are inconclusive, being neither demonstrable by reasoning nor deducible from experience.

267. In examining Mr Hume's argument on this subject, Dr Reid admits that the inferences we make of design from its effects are not the result of reasoning or of experience; but still he contends that such inferences may be made with a degree of certainty equal to what the human mind is able to attain in any instance whatever. The opinions we form of the talents of other men, nay, our belief that other men are intelligent beings, are founded on this very inference of design from its effects. Intelligence and design are not objects of our senses, and yet we judge of them every moment from external conduct and behaviour, with as little hesitation as we pronounce on the existence of what we immediately perceive.

268. Other philosophers have opposed the major proposition of the syllogism by an argument somewhat different.—In order to judge of the wisdom of any design, it is necessary (they observe) to know, first, what end the artist proposes to himself, and then to examine the means which he has employed to accomplish it. But in the universe all we see is, that certain things *are* accomplished, without having an opportunity of comparing them with a plan previously proposed.—A stone thrown at random must necessarily hit one object or another. When we see, therefore, such an effect produced, we are not entitled, independently of other information, to praise the dexterity of the marksman.

269. Among a great variety of considerations which might be urged in reply to this objection, the following seem to deserve particular attention.

(1.) Although from a single effect we may not be entitled to infer intelligence in the cause, yet the case is different when we see a number of causes conspiring to *one* end. We here see not only that an effect takes place, but have an intuitive conviction that this was the very effect intended. From seeing a single stone strike an object, we may not be authorized to conclude that this was the object aimed at. But what conclusion should we draw, if we saw the same object invariably hit by a number of stones thrown in succession?

(2.) A multiplicity of cases might be mentioned, in which we have really an opportunity of comparing the wisdom of nature with the ends to which it is directed. Of this many remarkable examples occur in the economy of the human body. When any accident or disease injures our frame, it is well known that the body possesses within itself a power of alleviating or remedying the evil. In such instances, we not only see an effect produced, but we see the operation of natural causes directed to the particular purpose of restoring the healthful state of the system.

(3.) There are many cases, particularly in the animal economy, in which the same effect is produced in different instances by very different means; and in which, of consequence, we have an opportunity of comparing the wisdom of Nature with the ends she has in view. "Art and means (says Baxter) are designedly multiplied, that we might not take it for the effect of chance: and in some cases the method itself is different, that we might see it is not the effect of surd necessity."—The science of comparative anatomy furnishes beautiful confirmations of the foregoing doctrine. From observing the effect produced by a particular organ in the case of any one animal, we might not perhaps be warranted to conclude that it was in order to produce this effect that the organ was contrived. But when, in the case of different species of animals, we see the same effect brought about by means extremely different, it is impossible for us to doubt that it was this common end which in all these instances Nature had in view.—Nor is this all. In comparing the anatomy of different tribes of animals, we find that the differences observable in their structure have a reference to their way of life and the habits for which they are destined; so that, from knowing the latter, we might be able in particular cases to frame conjectures *à priori* concerning the former.

270. From the foregoing hints it sufficiently appears that design may be inferred from its effects; and, also, that design may be traced in various parts of the universe from an actual examination of the means employed to accomplish particular ends.—Another inquiry, however, and a still more important, remains,—to consider the characters of this design as it is displayed in the universe; or, in other words,

to consider how far the design seems to indicate Wisdom; and whether it seems to operate in conformity to one uniform plan. The first investigation is useful by its tendency to elevate our conceptions of the Supreme Being; and the second is necessary for the demonstration of his Unity.

271. The study of philosophy in all its various branches, both natural and moral, affords at every step a new illustration of the subject to which these investigations relate; insomuch that the truths of natural religion gain an accession of evidence from every addition that is made to the stock of human knowledge. Hence, in the case of those individuals who devote themselves with fair and candid minds to the pursuits of science there is a gradual progress of light and conviction, keeping pace with the enlargement of their information and of their views; and hence a strong presumption that the influence which these truths have, even in the present state of society, on the minds of the multitude will continually increase, in proportion as the order of the material universe shall be more fully displayed by the discoveries of philosophy, and as the plan of Providence in the administration of human affairs shall be more completely unfolded in the future history of our species.

272. In considering the universe with a view to the illustration of the wisdom and unity of God, it is, in a peculiar degree, satisfactory to trace the relations which different parts of it bear to each other, and to remark the concurrence of things apparently unconnected and even remote, in promoting the same benevolent purposes. The following hints may be of use in suggesting reflections on this subject.

(1.) The adaptation of the bodies and of the instincts of animals to the laws of the material world:—of the organs of respiration, for example, and of the instinct of suction to the properties of the atmosphere;—of the *momentum* of light to the sensibility of the retina;—of the fabric of the eye to the laws of refraction;—of the size and strength of animals and vegetables to the laws of gravitation and of cohesion.

(2.) The adaptation of the bodies and of the instincts of animals to those particular climates and districts of the earth for which they are destined.

(3.) The relations subsisting between particular animals and particular vegetables; the latter furnishing to the former, salutary food in their healthful state, and useful remedies in the case of disease.

(4.) The connection which appears from the pneumatical discoveries of modern chemistry to exist between the processes of nature in the animal and in the vegetable kingdoms.

(5.) The relations which different tribes of animals bear to each other; one tribe being the natural prey of another, and each of them having their instruments of offence or defence provided accordingly.

(6.) The relations which the periodical instincts of migrating animals bear to the state of the season and to the vegetable productions of different parts of the globe.

273. This view of the subject is peculiarly striking, when we consider the relations which subsist between the nature of man and the circumstances of his external situation. An examination of his perceptive faculties in particular, and of his intellectual powers, as they are adapted to the structure and to the laws of the material world, opens a wide field of curious speculation.

274. The accommodation of the objects around him to his appetites, to his physical wants, and to his capacities of enjoyment, is no less wonderful; and exceeds so far what we observe in the case of other animals, as to authorise us to conclude that it was chiefly with a view to his happiness and improvement that the arrangements of this lower world were made.

275. There is another view of nature which tends remarkably to illustrate that unity of design which is the foundation of our belief of the unity of God;—to trace the analogies which are observable between the different departments of the universe which fall under our notice.—Of such analogies many instances may be derived from a comparative examination, 1. Of the structures of different tribes of animals; 2. Of the animal and of the vegetable kingdoms; and, 3. Of the various laws which regulate the phenomena of the material world.

276. It is pleasing to consider that this uniform and regular plan has been found to extend to the remotest limits to which the inquiries of philosophers have reached. The ancients in general supposed that the phenomena of the

heavens were regulated by laws perfectly unlike those which obtain within the circle of our experience. The modern discoveries have shown how widely they were mistaken; and indeed it was a conjecture *à priori*, that their ideas on this subject might perhaps be erroneous, which led the way to the theory of gravitation. Every subsequent discovery has confirmed the conjecture.

277. Nor is it only the more general laws of terrestrial bodies which extend to the remote parts of the universe. There is some ground for suspecting that the particular arrangements of things on the surfaces of the different planets are not wholly unlike those which we observe on our own.

278. Amusing and interesting as these physical speculations may be, it is still more delightful to trace the uniformity of design which is displayed in the *moral* world;—to compare the instincts of men with those of the brutes, and the instincts of the different tribes of the brutes with each other; and to remark, amidst the astonishing variety of means which are employed to accomplish the same ends, a certain analogy characterise them all;—or to observe in the minds of different individuals of our own species the workings of the same affections and passions, and to trace the uniformity of their operation in men of different ages and countries.— It is this which gives the great charm to what we call *nature* in the epic and dramatic composition; when the poet speaks a language to which every heart is an echo, and which, amidst all the effects of education and fashion in modifying and disguising the principles of our constitution, reminds all the various classes of readers or of spectators of the existence of those moral ties which unite us to each other, and to our common Parent.

279. Before leaving this subject, it is proper to remark that the metaphysical reasonings which have been occasionally employed in the illustration of it, ought not to be considered as forming any part of the argument for the existence of God, which (as was already observed) is an immediate and necessary consequence of the two principles formerly mentioned (§ 251). The scope of these reasonings is not to confirm the truth of the proposition, but to obviate the sceptical cavils which have been urged against it.

280. Reasoning and reflection are indeed necessary to

raise the mind to worthy conceptions of the Divine attributes, and to cure it of those prejudices which arise from limited and erroneous views of nature. While men confine their attention to detached and insulated appearances, Polytheism offers itself as the most natural creed; and it is only by slow and gradual steps that philosophy discovers to us those magnificent views of the universe which connect together all events, both physical and moral, as parts of *one* system and conspiring to *one* end.

281. Beside the sceptical objections already mentioned to the speculation concerning Final Causes, some others have been proposed with very different views. Des Cartes, in particular, taking for granted the existence of God as sufficiently established by other proofs, has rejected altogether this speculation from philosophy, as an impious and absurd attempt to penetrate into the designs of Providence. Some observations, much to the same purpose, occur in the works of Maupertuis and of Buffon.—To this class of objections against Final Causes a satisfactory answer is given by Mr Boyle, in an essay written expressly on the subject.

282. The authority of Lord Bacon has been frequently quoted in support of the opinion of these French philosophers. But if his writings be carefully examined, it will be found that the censures he bestows on Aristotle and his followers for their conjectures concerning the ends and intentions of Nature, are applicable only to the abuse of this doctrine in the Peripatetic school. It is a doctrine, according to them, which belongs properly to metaphysics or to natural theology, and not to natural philosophy; and which contributed much to mislead the Peripatetics in their physical inquiries. In a work of which it was the principal aim to explain the true plan of philosophical investigation, it was necessary to point out the absurdity of blending physical and final causes together, and of substituting conjectures concerning the intentions of Nature for an account of her operations. Perhaps it was prudent even to recommend the total exclusion of such conjectures from physics, in an age when the just rules of inquiry were so imperfectly understood.—

That Bacon did not mean to censure the speculation about Final Causes, when confined to its proper place and applied to its proper purpose, appears clearly from a variety of particular passages, as well as from the general strain and tendency of his writings.

283. In the present age, when the true method of philosophizing in physics is pretty generally understood, it does not seem to be so necessary as formerly to banish Final Causes from that branch of science; provided always they be kept distinct from Physical Causes, with which there is now but little danger of their being unwarily confounded. If this caution be attended to, the consideration of Final Causes, so far from leading us astray, may frequently be of use in guiding our researches.—It is, in fact, a mode of reasoning familiar to every philosopher, whatever his speculative opinions on the subject of natural religion may be. Thus, in the study of anatomy every man proceeds on the maxim that nothing in the body of an animal was made in vain; and when he meets with a part of which the use is not obvious, he feels himself dissatisfied till he discovers some, at least, of the purposes to which it is subservient. "I remember (says Mr Boyle) that when I asked our famous Harvey what were the things that induced him to think of a circulation of the blood? he answered me, that when he took notice that the valves in the veins of so many parts of the body were so placed that they gave a free passage to the blood towards the heart, but opposed the passage of the venal blood the contrary way; he was invited to imagine that so provident a cause as Nature had not placed so many valves without design; and no design seemed more probable than that, since the blood could not well, because of the interposing valves, be sent by the veins to the limbs, it should be sent through the arteries, and return through the veins, whose valves did not oppose its course that way."

284. An explanation of the use and abuse of the speculation concerning Final Causes, in the study of natural philosophy, is still a *desideratum* in science, and would form an important addition to that branch of logic which professes to state the rules of philosophical investigation.

SECTION I.

Of the Duties which respect the Deity.

PRELIMINARY INQUIRY INTO THE PRINCIPLES OF NATURAL RELIGION.

ARTICLE SECOND.
OF THE MORAL ATTRIBUTES OF THE DEITY.

285. The observations made in the last Article contain some of the principal heads of the argument for the existence of God; and also for his unity, for his power, and for his wisdom. Of the two last of these attributes we justly say that they are *infinite;* that is, that our imagination can set no bounds to them, and that our conceptions of them always rise in proportion as our faculties are cultivated, and as our knowledge of the universe becomes more extensive. The writers on Natural Religion commonly give a particular enumeration of attributes, which they divide into the natural, the intellectual, and the moral; and of which they treat at length in a systematical manner. This view of the subject, whatever may be its advantages, could not be adopted with propriety here. The remarks which follow are confined to the evidences of the Divine goodness and justice;—those attributes which constitute the moral perfection of the Deity, and which render him a proper object of religious worship.

I. *Of the Evidences of Benevolent Design in the Universe.*

286. Our ideas of the moral attributes of God must be derived from our own moral perceptions. It is only by attending to these that we can form a conception of what his attributes are; and it is in this way we are furnished with the strongest proofs that they really belong to him.

287. The peculiar sentiment of approbation with which we regard the virtue of beneficence in others, and the peculiar satisfaction with which we reflect on such of our own actions as have contributed to the happiness of mankind, to which we may add the exquisite pleasure accompanying the exercise of all the kind affections, naturally lead us to consider benevo-

lence or goodness as the supreme attribute of the Deity.—It is difficult, indeed, to conceive what other motive could have induced a Being, completely and independently happy, to have called his creatures into existence.

288. In this manner, without any examination of the fact, we have a strong presumption for the goodness of the Deity, and it is only after establishing this presumption *à priori*, that we can proceed to examine the fact with safety. It is true, indeed, that, independently of this presumption, the disorders we see would not demonstrate ill intention in the Author of the universe; as it would be still possible that these might contribute to the happiness and the perfection of the whole system.—But the contrary supposition would be equally possible, that there is nothing absolutely good in the universe, and that the communication of suffering is the ultimate end of the laws by which it is governed.

289. The argument for the goodness of God, derived from our own moral constitution, and strengthened by the consideration of our ignorance of the plans of Providence, affords an answer to all the objections which have been urged against this attribute of the Deity.—And the answer is conclusive, whatever the state of the fact may be with respect to the magnitude of the evils of which we complain.

290. But although this answer might silence our objections, something more is requisite, on a subject so momentous, to support our confidence and to animate our hopes. If no account could be given of the evils of life, but that they may possibly be good relatively to the whole universe;—still more, if it should appear that the sufferings of life overbalance its enjoyments; it could hardly be expected that any speculative reasoning would have much effect in banishing the melancholy suggestions of scepticism.—We are therefore naturally led, in the first place, to inquire whether some explanation may not be given of the origin of evil from a consideration of the facts which fall under our notice? and, secondly, to compare together the happiness and the misery which the world exhibits.

291. The question concerning the origin of evil has from the earliest times employed the ingenuity of speculative men, and various theories have been proposed to solve the difficulty. The most celebrated of these are the following.

(1.) The doctrine of Pre-existence.
(2.) The doctrine of the Manicheans.
(3.) The doctrine of Optimism.

292. According to the first hypothesis, the evils we suffer at present are punishments and expiations of moral delinquencies committed in a former stage of our being. This hypothesis, it is obvious (to mention no other objection), only removes the difficulty a little out of sight, without affording any explanation of it.

293. The Manicheans account for the mixture of good and evil in the universe, by the opposite agencies of two co-eternal and independent principles. Their doctrine has been examined and refuted by many authors, by reasonings *à priori;* but the most satisfactory of all the refutations is its obvious inconsistency with that unity of design which is everywhere conspicuous in nature.

294. The fundamental principle of the Optimists is, that all events are ordered for the best; and that the evils which we suffer are parts of a great system conducted by almighty power, under the direction of infinite wisdom and goodness.

295. Under this general title, however, are comprehended two very different descriptions of philosophers; those who admit and those who deny the freedom of human actions. The former only contend that everything is right so far as it is the work of God; and endeavour to show that the creation of beings endowed with free-will, and consequently liable to moral delinquency—and the government of the world by general laws from which occasional evils must result—furnish no solid objection to the perfection of the universe. But they hold at the same time that, although the permission of moral evil does not detract from the goodness of God, it is nevertheless imputable to man as a fault, and renders him justly obnoxious to punishment. This was the system of Plato, and of the best of the ancient philosophers, who in most instances state their doctrine in a manner perfectly consistent with man's free-will and moral agency.

296. By some modern authors the scheme of Optimism has been proposed in a form inconsistent with these suppositions, and which leads to a justification of moral evil, even with respect to the delinquent.

297. It is of great importance to attend to the distinction between these two systems; because it is customary among sceptical writers to confound them studiously together in order to extend to both that ridicule to which the latter is justly entitled.—The scope of the argument, as stated in the former system, may be collected from the following hints.

298. All the different subjects of human complaint may be reduced to two classes; Moral and Physical evils. The former comprehends those which arise from the abuse of Free-will; the latter those which result from the established laws of nature, and which man cannot prevent by his own efforts.

299. According to the definition now given of moral evil, the question with respect to its permission is reduced to this; Why was man made a free agent? A question to which it seems to be a sufficient reply: That perhaps the object of the Deity, in the government of the world, is not merely to communicate happiness, but to form his creatures to moral excellence;—or that the enjoyment of high degrees of happiness may perhaps necessarily require the previous acquisition of virtuous habits.

300. The sufferings produced by vice are, on this supposition, instances of the goodness of God, no less than the happiness resulting from virtue.

301. These observations justify Providence, not only for the permission of moral evil, but for the permission of many things which we commonly complain of as physical evils.—How great is the proportion of these, which are the obvious consequences of our vices and our prejudices; and which, so far from being a necessary part of the order of nature, seem intended to operate in the progress of human affairs, as a gradual remedy against the causes which produce them!

302. Some of our other complaints with respect to the lot of humanity will be found, on examination, to arise from partial views of the constitution of man, and from a want of attention to the circumstances which constitute his happiness, or promote his improvement.

303. Still, however, many evils remain, to which the foregoing principles do not apply. Such are those produced by what we commonly call the accidents of life;—accidents

from which no state of society, how perfect soever, can possibly be exempted; and which, if they be subservient to any benevolent purposes, contribute to none within the sphere of our knowledge.

304. Of this class of physical evils, the explanation must be derived from the general laws by which the government of the Deity appears to be conducted. The tendency of these laws will be found in every instance favourable to order and to happiness; and it is one of the noblest employments of philosophy to investigate the beneficent purposes to which they are subservient.—In a world, however, which is thus governed, and where the inhabitants are free agents, occasional inconveniences and misfortunes must unavoidably be incurred.

305. In the mean time, from this influence of "Time and Chance" on human affairs, salutary effects arise. Virtue is disinterested, and the characters of men are more completely displayed.

306. Many of our moral qualities, too, are the result of habits which imply the existence of physical evils. Patience, Fortitude, Humanity, all suppose a scene in which sufferings are to be endured in our own case, or relieved in the cases of others.

307. Thus it appears not only that partial evils *may be good* with respect to the whole system; but that their tendency *is* beneficial on the whole, even to that part of it which we see.

308. The argument for the goodness of God, which arises from the foregoing considerations, will be much strengthened, if it shall appear further that the sum of happiness in human life far exceeds the sum of misery.

309. In opposition to this conclusion, the prevalence of moral evil over moral good, in the characters of men, has been insisted on by many writers; and in proof of it an appeal has been made to the catalogue of crimes which sully the history of past ages.

310. Whatever opinion we may adopt with respect to the state of the fact in this particular instance; no objection can be drawn from it to the foregoing reasonings; for moral evil is alone imputable to the being by whom it is committed. There is, however, no necessity for having recourse to this

evasion. Corrupted as mankind are, the proportion of human life which is spent in vice is inconsiderable, when compared with the whole of its extent.—History itself is a proof of this; for the events it records are chiefly those which are calculated, by their singularity, to engage the curiosity and to interest the passions of the reader.—In computing, besides, the moral demerit of mankind from their external actions, a large allowance ought to be made for erroneous speculative opinions; for false conceptions of facts; for prejudices inspired by the influence of prevailing manners, and for habits contracted insensibly in early infancy.

311. With respect to the balance of physical evil and physical good, the argument is still clearer; if it be acknowledged (§ 304.), that the general laws of nature are beneficent in their tendency, and that the inconveniencies which arise from them are only occasional.

312. Of these occasional evils, too, no inconsiderable part may be traced to the obstacles which human institutions oppose to the order of things recommended by nature.—How chimerical soever the speculations of philosophers concerning the perfection of legislation may be, they are useful, at least, in illustrating the wisdom and goodness of the Divine government.

313. Nor is it only in those laws which regulate the more essential interests of mankind that a beneficent intention may be traced. What a rich provision is made for our enjoyment in the pleasures of the understanding, of the imagination, and of the heart; and how little do they depend on the caprice of fortune!—The positive accommodation of our sensitive powers to the scene we occupy is still more wonderful: —Of the organ of smell, for example, to the perfumes of the vegetable world; of the taste, to the endless profusion of luxuries which the earth, the air, and the waters afford; of the ear, to the melodies of the birds; of the eye, to all the beauties and glories of the visible creation.

314. Among these marks of beneficence in the frame of man, the constitution of his mind with respect to Habits must not be omitted. So great is their influence, that there is hardly any situation to which his wishes may not be gradually reconciled, nay, where he will not find himself, in time, more comfortable than in those which are looked up

to with envy by the bulk of mankind. By this power of accommodation to external circumstances a remedy is in part provided for the occasional evils resulting from the operation of general laws.

315. In judging of the feelings of those who are placed in situations very different from our own, due allowances are seldom made for the effects of habit; and, of consequence, our estimates of the happiness of life fall short greatly of the truth.

II. *Of the Evidences of the Moral Government of the Deity.*

316. It was before remarked (§ 286.), that as our first ideas of the moral attributes of God are derived from our own moral perceptions, so it is from the consideration of these that the strongest proofs of his attributes arise.

317. The distinction between Right and Wrong, as was formerly observed (§ 200.), is apprehended by the mind to be eternal and immutable, no less than the distinction between mathematical Truth and Falsehood. To argue therefore from our own moral judgments to the administration of the Deity, cannot be justly censured as a rash extension to the Divine nature of suggestions resulting from the arbitrary constitution of our own minds.

318. The power we have of conceiving this distinction is one of the most remarkable of those which raise us above the brutes, and the sense of obligation which it involves possesses a distinguished pre-eminence over all our other principles of action (§ 219.). To act in conformity to our sense of rectitude is plainly the highest excellence which our nature is capable of attaining; nor can we avoid extending the same rule of estimation to all intelligent beings whatever.

319. Besides these conclusions with respect to the Divine attributes (which seem to be implied in our very perception of moral distinctions), there are others perfectly agreeable to them which continually force themselves on the mind in the exercise of our moral judgments, both with respect to our own conduct and that of other men. The reverence which we feel to be due to the admonitions of Conscience; the sense of merit and demerit which accompanies our good and bad actions; the warm interest we take in the fortunes

of the virtuous; the indignation we feel at the occasional triumphs of successful villany,—all imply a secret conviction of the moral administration of the universe.

320. An examination of the ordinary course of human affairs adds to the force of these considerations, and furnishes a proof from the fact that, notwithstanding the seemingly promiscuous distribution of happiness and misery in this life, the reward of virtue and the punishment of vice are the great objects of all the general laws by which the world is governed. The disorders, in the mean time, which in such a world as ours cannot fail to arise in particular instances, when they are compared with our natural sense of good and of ill desert, afford a presumption that in a future state the moral government which we see begun here will be carried into complete execution.

SECTION I.

Of the Duties which respect the Deity.

PRELIMINARY INQUIRY INTO THE PRINCIPLES OF NATURAL RELIGION.

ARTICLE THIRD.

OF A FUTURE STATE.

321. THE consideration of the Divine attributes naturally leads our thoughts to the sequel of that plan of moral administration which may be traced distinctly amidst all the apparent disorders of our present condition; and which our own moral constitution, joined to our conclusions concerning the perfections of God, afford us the strongest intimations, will be more completely unfolded in some subsequent stage of our being. The doctrine indeed of a future state seems to be in a great measure implied in every system of religious relief; for why were we rendered capable of elevating our thoughts to the Deity, if all our hopes are to terminate here? or why were we furnished with powers which range through the infinity of space and of time, if our lot is to be

the same with that of the beasts which perish?—But although the doctrine of a future state be implied in every scheme of religion, the truths of religion are not necessarily implied in the doctrine of a future state. Even absolute Atheism does not destroy all the arguments for the immortality of the soul. Whether it be owing to an overruling intelligence or not, it is a *fact* which no man can deny, that there are general laws which regulate the course of human affairs, and that even in this world we see manifest indications of a connection between virtue and happiness.—Why may not *necessity* continue that existence it at first gave birth to? and why may not the connection between virtue and happiness subsist for ever?

I. *Of the Argument for a Future State derived from the Nature of Mind.*

322. In collecting the various evidences which the light of nature affords for a future state, too, much stress has commonly been laid upon the soul's Immateriality. The proper use of that doctrine is not to demonstrate that the soul is physically and necessarily immortal; but to refute the objections which have been urged against the possibility of its existing in a separate state from the body. Although our knowledge of the nature of Mind may not be sufficient to afford us any positive argument on the subject; yet, even if it can be shown that the dissolution of the body does not necessarily infer the extinction of the soul; and, still more, if it can be shown that the presumption is in favour of the contrary supposition, the moral proofs of a future retribution will meet with a more easy reception when the doctrine is freed from the metaphysical difficulties which it has been apprehended to involve.

323. It was before remarked (§ 28.), that our notions both of body and mind are merely relative; that we know the one only by its sensible qualities, and the other by the operations of which we are conscious.—To say, therefore, of Mind, that it is not material, is to affirm a proposition, the truth of which is involved in the only conceptions of Matter and of Mind that we are capable of forming.

324. The doubts that have been suggested, with respect

to the essential distinction between Matter and Mind, derive all their plausibility from the habits of inattention we acquire in early infancy to our mental operations. It was plainly the intention of Nature that our thoughts should be habitually directed to things external; and, accordingly, the bulk of mankind are not only indisposed to study the intellectual phenomena, but are incapable of that degree of reflection which is necessary for their examination. Hence it is, that when we begin to analyze our own internal constitution, we find the facts it presents to us so very intimately associated in our conceptions with the qualities of Matter, that it is impossible for us to draw distinctly and steadily the line between them; and that when Mind and Matter are concerned in the same event, the former is either entirely overlooked, or is regarded only as an accessory principle, dependent for its existence on the latter.—The tendency which all men have to refer the sensation of colour to the objects by which it is excited, may serve to illustrate the manner in which the qualities of mind and body come to be blended in our apprehensions.

325. If these remarks be well founded, the prejudices which give support to the scheme of Materialism are not likely to be cured by any metaphysical reasonings, how clear and conclusive soever, so long as the judgment continues to be warped by such obstinate associations as have just been mentioned. A habit of reflecting on the laws of thought, as they are to be collected from our own consciousness, together with a habit of resisting those illusions of the fancy which lead superficial inquirers to substitute analogies for facts, will gradually enable us to make the phenomena of Matter and those of Mind distinct objects of attention; and as soon as this happens the absurdity of Materialism must appear intuitively obvious.

326. It is entirely owing to our early familiarity with material objects, and our early habits of inattention to what passes within us, that Materialism is apt to appear at first sight to be less absurd than the opposite system, which represents *Mind* as the only existence in the universe. Of the two doctrines, that of Berkeley is at once the safest and the most philosophical; not only as it contradicts merely the suggestions of our perceptions, while the other contra-

dicts the suggestions of our consciousness; but as various plausible arguments may be urged in its favour, from the phenomena of dreaming; whereas no instance can be mentioned in which sensation and intelligence appear to result from any combination of the particles of Matter.

327. Besides the evidences for the existence of Mind which our own consciousness affords, and those which are exhibited by other men, and by the lower animals, there are many presented to us by every part of the material world. We are so constituted that every change in it we see suggests to us the notion of an efficient cause;—and every combination of means conspiring to an end suggests to us the notion of intelligence. And, accordingly, the various changes which take place in nature, and the order and beauty of the universe, have in every age been regarded as the effects of power and wisdom; that is, of the operation of Mind. In the material world, therefore, as well as in the case of animated nature, we are led to conceive Body as a passive subject, and Mind as the moving and governing agent. And it deserves attention, that in the former class of phenomena Mind appears to move and arrange the parts of matter without being united with it, as in the case of animal life.

328. There are various circumstances which render it highly probable that the union between soul and body, which takes place in our present state, so far from being essential to the exercise of our powers and faculties, was intended to limit the sphere of our information; and to prevent us from acquiring in this early stage of our being too clear a view of the constitution and government of the universe. Indeed, when we reflect on the difference between the operations of Mind and the qualities of Matter, it appears much more wonderful that the two substances should be so intimately united as we find them actually to be, than to suppose that the former may exist in a conscious and intelligent state when separated from the latter.

329. The most plausible objections. nevertheless, to the doctrine of a future state, have been drawn from the intimacy of this union. From the effects of intoxication, madness, and other diseases, it appears that a certain condition of the body is necessary to the intellectual operations; and in the case of old men, it is generally found that a decline

of the faculties keeps pace with the decay of bodily health and vigour. The few exceptions that occur to the universality of this fact only prove that there are some diseases fatal to life which do not injure those parts of the body with which the intellectual operations are more immediately connected.

330. The reply which Cicero has made to these objections is equally ingenious and solid. "Suppose a person to have been educated from his infancy in a chamber where he enjoyed no opportunity of seeing external objects but through a small chink in the window-shutter; would he not be apt to consider this chink as essential to his vision? and would it not be difficult to persuade him that his prospects would be enlarged by demolishing the walls of his prison?" Admitting that this analogy is founded merely on fancy; yet, if it be granted that there is no absurdity in the supposition, it furnishes a sufficient answer to all the reasonings which have been stated against the possibility of the soul's separate existence, from the consideration of its present union with the body.

331. In support of the foregoing conclusions, many strong arguments might be derived from an accurate examination and analysis of our ideas of Matter and its qualities. But such speculations could not be rendered intelligible, without a previous explanation of some principles too abstruse to be introduced here.

II. *Of the Evidences for a Future State arising from the Human Constitution, and from the circumstances in which Man is placed.*

332. The great extent of this subject necessarily confines the following remarks to an enumeration of the principal heads of the argument. These are stated without any illustration.

(1.) The natural desire of immortality, and the anticipations of futurity inspired by hope.

(2.) The natural apprehensions of the mind when under the influence of remorse.

(3.) The exact accommodation of the condition of the lower animals to their instincts and their sensitive powers;—

contrasted with the unsuitableness of the present state of things to the intellectual faculties of man,—to his capacities of enjoyment,—and to the conceptions of happiness and of perfection which he is able to form.

(4.) The foundation which is laid in the principles of our constitution for a progressive and an unlimited improvement.

(5.) The information we are rendered capable of acquiring concerning the more remote parts of the universe; the unlimited range which is opened to the human imagination through the immensity of space and of time; and the ideas, however imperfect, which philosophy affords us of the existence and attributes of an over-ruling Mind:—Acquisitions for which an obvious final cause may be traced, on the supposition of a future state; but which, if that supposition be rejected, could have no other effect than to make the business of life appear unworthy of our regard.

(6.) The tendency of the infirmities of age and of the pains of disease to strengthen and confirm our moral habits; and the difficulty of accounting, upon the hypothesis of annihilation, for those sufferings which commonly put a period to the existence of man.

(7.) The discordance between our moral judgments and feelings, and the course of human affairs.

(8.) The analogy of the material world; in some parts of which the most complete and the most systematical order may be traced, and of which our views always become the more satisfactory the wider our knowledge extends. It is the supposition of a future state alone that can furnish a key to the present disorders of the moral world; and without it many of the most striking phenomena of human life must remain for ever inexplicable.

(9.) The inconsistency of supposing that the moral laws which regulate the course of human affairs have no reference to anything beyond the limits of the present scene; when all the bodies which compose the visible universe appear to be related to each other, as parts of one great physical system.

333. Of the different considerations now mentioned, there is not one, perhaps, which, taken singly, would be sufficient to establish the truth they are brought to prove; but taken in conjunction, their force appears irresistible. They not

only all terminate in the same conclusion, but they mutually reflect light on each other; and they have that sort of consistency and connection among themselves which could hardly be supposed to take place among a series of false propositions.

334. The same remark may be extended to the other principles of Natural Religion. They all hang together in such a manner, that if one of them be granted it facilitates the way for the reception of the rest.

335. Nor is it merely with each other that these principles are connected. They have a relation to all the other principles of Moral Philosophy;—insomuch, that a person who entertains just views of the one never fails to entertain also just views of the other. Perhaps it would not be going too far to assert, that they have a relation to almost all the truths we know, in the moral, the intellectual, and the material worlds. One thing is certain, that in proportion as our knowledge extends, our doubts and objections disappear; new light continually breaks in upon us from every quarter, and more of order and system appears in the universe.

336. It is a strong confirmation of these remarks, that the most important discoveries, both in moral and physical science, have been made by men friendly to the principles of natural religion; and that those writers who have affected to be sceptical on this last subject have in general been paradoxical and sophistical in their other inquiries. This consideration, while it illustrates the connection which different classes of truth have with each other, proves that it is to a mind well fitted for the discovery and reception of truth in general that the evidences of Religion are the most satisfactory.

337. The influence which the belief of a future state has on the conduct and on the enjoyments of mankind also tends to confirm its credibility. This is so remarkable, that it has led some to consider it merely as an invention of politicians, to preserve the good order of society, and to support the feeble mind under the sufferings of human life. But if it be allowed that it has really such a tendency, can it be supposed that the Author of the universe should have left consequences so very momentous to depend on the belief of a chimera, which was in time to vanish before the light of

philosophy? Is it not more probable, that the enlargement of our knowledge, to which we are so powerfully prompted by the principle of curiosity, will tend to increase, and not to diminish, the virtue and the happiness of mankind; and instead of spreading a gloom over creation, and extinguishing the hopes which nature inspires, will gradually unfold to us in the moral world, the same order and beauty we admire in the material?

338. After the view which has been given of the principles of Natural Religion, little remains to be added concerning the duties which respect the Deity. To employ our faculties in studying those evidences of power, of wisdom, and of goodness, which he has displayed in his works; as it is the foundation, in other instances, of our sense of religious obligation; so it is in itself a duty incumbent on us, as reasonable and moral beings, capable of recognizing the existence of an Almighty Cause, and of feeling corresponding sentiments of devotion. By those who entertain just opinions on this most important of all subjects, the following practical consequences, which comprehend some of the chief effects of religion on the temper and conduct, will be readily admitted as self-evident propositions.

339. In the first place: If the Deity be possessed of infinite moral excellence we must feel towards him, in an infinite degree, all those affections of love, gratitude, and confidence, which are excited by the imperfect worth we observe among our fellow-creatures; for it is by conceiving all that is benevolent and amiable in man, raised to the highest perfection, that we can alone form some faint notion of the Divine nature.—To cultivate, therefore, an habitual love and reverence to the Supreme Being, may be justly considered as the first great branch of morality; nor is the virtue of that man complete, or even consistent with itself, in whose mind these sentiments of piety are wanting.

340. Secondly: Although Religion can with no propriety be considered as the sole foundation of morality, yet when we are convinced that God is infinitely good, and that he is the friend and protector of virtue, this belief affords the most powerful inducements to the practice of every branch of our duty. It leads us to consider conscience as the vicegerent

of God, and to attend to its suggestions as to the commands of that Being from whom we have received our existence, and the great object of whose government is to promote the happiness and the perfection of his whole creation.

341. Thirdly: A regard to our own happiness in the future stages of our being (which will be afterwards shown to constitute a moral obligation) ought to conspire with the other motives already mentioned in stimulating our virtuous exertions. The moral perceptions we have received from God, more particularly our sense of merit and demerit, may be considered as clear indications of future rewards and punishments, which, in due time, he will not fail to distribute. Religion is therefore a species of authoritative law, enforced by the most awful sanctions, and extending not merely to our actions, but to our thoughts.—In the case of the lower orders of men, who are incapable of abstract speculation, and whose moral feelings cannot be supposed to have received much cultivation; it is chiefly this view of Religion, which is addressed to their hopes and fears, that secures a faithful discharge of their social duties.

342. In the last place: A sense of Religion, where it is sincere, will necessarily be attended with a complete resignation of our own will to that of the Deity; as it teaches us to regard every event, even the most afflicting, as calculated to promote beneficent purposes which we are unable to comprehend; and to promote finally the perfection and happiness of our own nature.

SECTION II.

Of the Duties which respect our Fellow-creatures.

343. Under this title it is not proposed to give a complete enumeration of our social duties, but only to point out some of the most important; chiefly with a view to show the imperfection of those systems of morals which attempt to resolve the whole of virtue into one particular principle. Among these, that which resolves virtue into Benevolence is undoubtedly the most amiable; but even this system will appear, from the following remarks, to be not only inconsistent with truth, but to lead to dangerous consequences.

ARTICLE FIRST.

OF BENEVOLENCE.

344. It has been supposed by some moralists, that Benevolence is only the immediate object of moral approbation, and that the obligation of all our moral duties arises entirely from their apprehended tendency to promote the happiness of society.

345. Notwithstanding the various appearances in human nature, which seem at first view to favour this theory, it is liable to insurmountable objections. If the merit of an action depended on no other circumstance than the quantity of good intended by the agent, it would follow that the rectitude of an action could be in no case influenced by the mutual relations of the parties;—a conclusion directly contrary to the universal judgments of mankind, with respect to the obligations of Gratitude, of Veracity, and of Justice.

346. Unless we admit these duties to be immediately obligatory, we must admit the maxim, that a good end may sanctify whatever means are necessary for its accomplishment; or, in other words, that it would be lawful for us to dispense with the obligations of gratitude, of veracity, and of justice, whenever, by doing so, we had a prospect of promoting any of the essential interests of society.

347. It may perhaps be urged that a regard to utility would lead, in such cases, to an invariable adherence to general rules, because in this way more good is produced on the whole than could be obtained by any occasional deviations from them;—that it is this idea of utility which first leads us to approve of the different virtues, and that afterwards habit and the association of ideas make us observe their rules, without thinking of consequences. But is not this to adopt that mode of reasoning which the patrons of the Benevolent system have censured so severely in those philosophers who have attempted to deduce all our actions from Self-love; and may not the arguments they have employed against their adversaries be retorted upon themselves.

348. That the practice of veracity and justice, and of all our other duties, is useful to mankind, is acknowledged by

moralists of all descriptions; and there is good reason for believing that, if a person saw all the consequences of his actions, he would perceive that an adherence to their rules is useful and advantageous on the whole, even in those cases in which his limited views incline him to think otherwise. It is *possible* that, in the Deity, benevolence, or a regard to utility, may be the sole principle of action; and that the ultimate end for which he enjoined to his creatures the duties of veracity and justice was to secure their own happiness; but still, with respect to man, they are indispensable laws, for he has an immediate perception of their rectitude. And, indeed, if he had not, but were left to deduce their rectitude from the consequences which they have a tendency to produce, it may be doubted if there would be enough of virtue left in the world to hold society together.

349. These remarks are applicable to a considerable variety of moral systems, which have been offered to the world under very different forms, but which agree with each other in deriving the practical rules of virtuous conduct from considerations of Utility. All of these systems are but modifications of the old doctrine which resolves the whole of virtue into Benevolence.

350. But although Benevolence does not constitute the whole of our duty, it must be acknowledged to be, not only one of its most important branches, but the object of a very peculiar and enthusiastic admiration. The plausibility of the systems to which the preceding observations relate is a sufficient proof of the rank it is universally understood to hold among the virtues.

351. It may be proper to add, that the Benevolence which is an object of moral approbation is a fixed and settled disposition to promote the happiness of our fellow-creatures. It is peculiar to a rational nature, and is not to be confounded with those kind affections which are common to us with the brutes. These are subsidiary, in fact, to the principle of Benevolence; and they are always amiable qualities in a character: but, so far as they are constitutional, they are certainly in no respect meritorious. Where they are possessed in an eminent degree, we may perhaps consider them as a ground of moral esteem; because they indicate the pains which have been bestowed on their cultivation, and a course

of active virtue in which they have been exercised and strengthened. A person on the contrary who wants them is always an object of horror;—chiefly because we know that they are only to be eradicated by long habits of profligacy; and partly in consequence of the uneasiness we feel when we see the ordinary course of nature violated in any of her productions.

352. Some of the writers who resolve virtue into Benevolence have not attended sufficiently to this consideration. They frequently speak of virtuous and vicious affections; whereas these epithets belong not to affections, but to actions; or, still more properly, to the *dispositions* and *purposes* from which actions proceed.

353. Where a rational and settled Benevolence forms part of a character, it will render the conduct perfectly uniform, and will exclude the possibility of those inconsistencies that are frequently observable in individuals who give themselves up to the guidance of particular affections, either private or public. In truth, all those offices, whether apparently trifling or important, by which the happiness of other men is affected; Civility, Gentleness, Kindness, Humanity, Patriotism, Universal Benevolence; are only diversified expressions of the same disposition, according to the circumstances in which it operates, and the relations which the agent bears to others.

ARTICLE SECOND.

OF JUSTICE.

354. The word Justice, in its most extensive signification, denotes that disposition which leads us, in cases where our own temper, or passions, or interest are concerned, to determine and to act, without being biassed by partial considerations.

355. In order to free our minds from the influence of these, experience teaches us either to recollect the judgments we have formerly passed in similar circumstances on the conduct of others; or to state cases to ourselves, in which we, and all our personal concerns, are left entirely out of the question.

356. But although expedients of this sort are necessary to the best of men, for correcting their moral judgments upon questions in which they themselves are parties, it will not therefore follow (as some have supposed),* that our only ideas of right and wrong, with respect to our own conduct, are derived from our sentiments with respect to the conduct of others. The intention of such expedients is merely to obtain a just and fair view of circumstances; and after this view has been obtained, the question still remains, what constitutes the obligation upon us to act in a particular manner? For it is of great consequence to remark, that when we have once satisfied ourselves with respect to the conduct which an impartial judge would approve of, we feel that this conduct is *right* for us, and that we are under a moral obligation to act accordingly. If we had had recourse to no expedient for correcting our first judgment, we should still have formed some judgment or other of a particular conduct, as right, wrong, or indifferent; and the only difference would have been, that we should probably have decided erroneously from a false or a partial view of the case.

357. As it would be endless to attempt to point out all the various forms in which the disposition of Justice may display itself in life, it is necessary to confine our attention to a few of its more important effects. These may be arranged under two heads, according as it operates,—1st, in restraining the partialities of the temper and of the passions, and 2nd, in restraining the partialities of selfishness where a competition takes place between our interests and those of other men. These two modifications of Justice may be distinguished from each other by calling the first *Candour* and the second *Uprightness* or *Integrity*.

I. *Of Candour.*

358. This disposition may be considered in three points of view; as it is displayed,
    (1.) In judging of the talents of others.
    (2.) In judging of their intentions.
    (3.) In controversy.

---

* See Mr. Smith's Theory of Moral Sentiment.

359. The difficulty of estimating candidly the Talents of other men arises, in a great measure, from the tendency of emulation to degenerate into envy. Notwithstanding the reality of the theoretical distinction between these dispositions of mind (§ 139.), it is certain that in practice nothing is more arduous than to realize it completely, and to check that self-partiality which, while it leads us to dwell on our own personal advantages, and to magnify them in our own estimation, prevents us either from attending sufficiently to the merits of others, or from viewing them in the most favourable light. Of all this a good man will soon be satisfied from his own experience; and he will endeavour to guard against it as far as he is able by judging of the pretensions of a rival, or even of an enemy, as he would have done if there had been no interference between his claims and theirs. In other words, he will endeavour to do Justice to their merits, and to bring himself, if possible, to love and to honour that genius and ability which have eclipsed his own.—Nor will he retire in disgust from the race because he has been outstripped by others, but will redouble all his exertions in the service of mankind; recollecting that if nature has been more partial to others than to him in her intellectual gifts, she has left open to all the theatre of Virtue. where the merits of individuals are determined, not by their actual attainments, but by the use and improvement they make of those advantages which their situation has afforded them.

360. Candour, in judging of the Intentions of others, is a disposition of still greater importance.—Several considerations were formerly suggested (§ 310.) which render it highly probable that there is much less vice or criminal intention in the world than is commonly imagined; and that the greater part of the disputes among mankind arise from mutual mistake or misapprehension. It is but an instance, then, of that Justice we owe to others, to make the most candid allowances for their apparent deviations, and to give every action the most favourable construction it can possibly admit of.—Such a temper, while it renders a man respectable and amiable in society, contributes, perhaps more than any other circumstance, to his private happiness.

361. Candour in Controversy implies a strong sense of Justice, united to disinterested love of Truth; two qualities

which are so nearly allied that they can scarcely be supposed to exist separately. The latter guards the mind against error in its solitary speculations; the former imposes an additional check when the irritation of dispute disturbs the cool exercise of the understanding. Where they are thus displayed in their joint effect, they evince the purity of that moral rectitude in which the essence of both consists; but so rarely is this combination exhibited in human life, even in the character of those who maintain the fairest reputation for Justice and for Veracity, as to warrant the conclusion, that these virtues (so effectually secured to a certain extent by compulsory law, or by public opinion) are, in a moral view, of fully as difficult attainment as any of the others.

362. The foregoing illustrations are stated at some length, in order to correct those partial definitions of Justice which restrict its province to a rigorous observance of the rules of Integrity or Honesty in our dealings with our fellow-creatures. So far as this last disposition proceeds from a sense of duty, uninfluenced by human laws, it coincides exactly with that branch of Virtue which has been now described under the title of Candour.

II. *Of Uprightness or Integrity.*

363. These words are commonly employed to express that disposition of mind which leads us to observe the rules of Justice in cases where our interest is supposed to interfere with the rights of other men; a branch of Justice so important that it has, in a great measure, appropriated the name to itself.—The observations made by Mr Hume and Mr Smith on the differences between Justice and the other virtues, apply only to this last branch of it; and it is this branch which properly forms the subject of that part of Ethics which is called Natural Jurisprudence. In the remaining paragraphs of this article, when the word Justice occurs it is to be understood in the limited sense now mentioned.

364. The circumstances which distinguish Justice from the other virtues are chiefly two. In the first place, its rules may be laid down with a degree of accuracy of which

moral precepts do not in any other instance admit.* Secondly, its rules may be enforced, inasmuch as every breach of them violates the rights of some other person, and entitles him to employ force for his defence or security.

365. Another distinction between Justice and the other virtues is much insisted on by Mr Hume. It is, according to him, an artificial and not a natural virtue; and derives all its obligations from the political union, and from considerations of utility.

366. The principal argument alleged in support of this proposition is, that there is no implanted principle prompting us by a blind impulse to the exercise of Justice, similar to those affections which conspire with and strengthen our benevolent dispositions.

367. But, granting the fact upon which this argument proceeds, nothing can be inferred from it that makes an essential distinction between the obligations of Justice and of Beneficence; for so far as we act merely from the blind impulse of an affection our conduct cannot be considered as virtuous. Our affections were given us to arrest our attention to particular objects whose happiness is connected with our exertions; and to excite and support the activity of the mind when a sense of duty might be insufficient for the purpose: but the propriety or impropriety of our conduct depends in no instance on the strength or weakness of the affection, but on our obeying or disobeying the dictates of reason and of conscience. These inform us, in language which it is impossible to mistake, that it is sometimes a duty to check the most amiable and pleasing emotions of the heart;—to withdraw, for example, from the sight of those distresses which stronger claims forbid us to relieve, and to deny ourselves that exquisite luxury which arises from the exercise of humanity.—So far, therefore, as Benevolence is a virtue, it is precisely on the same footing with Justice; that is, we approve of it not because it is agreeable to us, but because we feel it to be a duty.

368. It may be further remarked, That there are very strong implanted principles which serve as checks on In-

* Theory of Moral Sentiments.

justice; the principles, to wit, of Resentment and of Indignation, which are surely as much a part of the human constitution as pity or parental affection. — That these principles imply a sense of Injustice, and consequently of Justice, was formerly observed (§ 155).

369. In one remarkable instance, too, Nature has made an additional provision for keeping alive among men a sense of those obligations which Justice imposes. That the good offices which we have received from others constitute a Debt which it is morally incumbent on us to discharge by all lawful means in our power, is acknowledged in the common forms of expression employed on such occasions, both by philosophers and the vulgar. As the obligations of Gratitude, however, do not admit (like the rules of honesty, strictly so called) of support from the magistrate, Nature has judged it proper to enforce their observance by one of the most irresistible and delightful impulses of the human frame. According to this view of the subject, Gratitude, considered as a moral duty, is a branch of Justice, recommended to us in a peculiar manner by those pleasing emotions which accompany all the modes of benevolent affection. It is at the same time a branch of what was formerly called rational benevolence; not interfering with the duty we owe to mankind in general, but tending in a variety of respects to augment the sum of social happiness. The casuistical questions to which this part of Ethics has given rise, however perplexing some of them may appear in theory, seldom, if ever, occasion any hesitation in the conduct of those to whom a sense of duty is the acknowledged rule of action: —Such is the harmony among all the various parts of our constitution, when subjected to the control of reason and conscience, and so nearly allied are the dispositions which prompt to the different offices of a virtuous life.

370. As the rules of Justice, when applied to questions involving the rights of other men, admit in their statement of a degree of accuracy peculiar to themselves, that part of Ethics which relates to them has been formed, in modern times, into a separate branch of the science, under the title of Natural Jurisprudence.

371. The manner in which this subject has been hitherto treated has been much influenced by the professional habits

of those who first turned their attention to it. Not only have its principles been delivered in the form of a system of law, but the technical language and the arbitrary arrangements of the Roman code have been servilely copied.

372. In consequence of this, an important branch of the law of nature has gradually assumed an artificial and scholastic appearance; and many capricious maxims have insensibly mingled themselves with the principles of universal jurisprudence.—Hence, too, the frivolous discussions with respect to minute and imaginary questions which so often occupy the place of those general and fundamental disquisitions that are suggested by the common nature and the common circumstances of the human race.

373. And still more material inconvenience has resulted from the professional habits of the earliest writers on jurisprudence. Not contented with stating the rules of Justice in that form and language which was most familiar to their own minds, they have attempted to extend the same plan to all the other branches of Moral Philosophy; and, by the help of arbitrary definitions, to supersede the necessity of accommodating their modes of inquiry to the various nature of their subject. Although Justice is the only branch of Virtue in which there is always a Right on the one hand corresponding to an Obligation on the other, they have contrived, by fictions of Imperfect and of External Rights, to treat indirectly of all our different duties, by pointing out the rights which are supposed to be their correlates. It is chiefly owing to this, that a study, which in the writings of the ancients is the most engaging and the most useful of any, has become in so great a proportion of modern systems as uninviting and almost as useless as the logic of the school-men.

374. Besides these defects in the modern systems of jurisprudence, (defects produced by the accidental habits of those who first cultivated the study,) there is another essential one arising from the inaccurate conceptions which have been formed of the object of the science. Although the obligations of Justice are by no means resolvable into considerations of Utility, yet, in every political association, they are so blended together in the institutions of men that it is impossible for us to separate them completely in our reasonings; and accordingly (as Mr Hume has remarked)

the writers on jurisprudence, while they profess to confine themselves entirely to the former, are continually taking principles for granted which have a reference to the latter. It seems therefore to be proper, instead of treating of jurisprudence merely as a system of natural justice, to unite it with politics; and to illustrate the general principles of Justice and of Expediency as they are actually combined in the constitution of society. This view of the subject (which according to the arrangement formerly mentioned (§ 2.) belongs to the third part of Moral Philosophy) will show, at the same time, how wonderfully these principles coincide in their applications; and how partial those conceptions of utility are which have so often led politicians to depart from what they felt to be just in quest of what their limited judgment apprehended to be expedient.

ARTICLE THIRD.

Of Veracity

375. The important rank which Veracity holds among our social duties appears from the obvious consequences that would result if no foundation were laid for it in the constitution of our nature.—The purposes of speech would be frustrated, and every man's opportunities of knowledge would be limited to his own personal experience.

376. Considerations of utility, however, do not seem to be the only ground of the approbation we bestow on this disposition. Abstracting from all regard to consequences, there is something pleasing and amiable in sincerity, openness, and truth; something disagreeable and disgusting in duplicity, equivocation, and falsehood. Dr Hutcheson himself, the great patron of that theory which resolves all moral qualities into Benevolence, confesses this; for he speaks of a *sense* which leads us to approve of Veracity, distinct from the *sense* which approves of qualities useful to mankind.* As this, however, is at best but a vague way of speaking, it may be proper to analyze more particularly that part of

* Phil. Moral. Instit. compend.

our constitution from which our approbation of Veracity arises.

377. That there is in the human mind a natural or instinctive principle of Veracity, has been remarked by many authors;—the same part of our constitution which prompts to social intercourse prompting also to sincerity in our mutual communications. Truth is always the spontaneous and native expression of our sentiments; whereas, Falsehood implies a certain violence done to our nature in consequence of the influence of some motive which we are anxious to conceal.

378. Corresponding to this instinctive principle of Veracity, there is a principle (coeval with the use of language) determining us to repose faith in testimony.* Without such a disposition, the education of children would be impracticable; and accordingly, so far from being the result of experience, it seems to be, in the first instance, unlimited; nature intrusting its gradual correction to the progress of reason and of observation. It bears a striking analogy, both in its origin and in its final cause, to our instinctive expectation of the continuance of those laws which regulate the course of physical events (71.) (3.).

379. In infancy, the former principle is by no means so conspicuous as the latter; and it sometimes happens that a good deal of care is necessary to cherish it.—But in such cases, it will always be found that there is some indirect motive combined with the desire of social communication; such as Fear, or Vanity, or Mischief, or Sensuality.—An habitual disposition, therefore, to deceit, may be considered as an infallible symptom of some more remote, and perhaps less palpable, evil, disordering the moral constitution. It is only by detecting and removing this radical fault that its pernicious consequences can be corrected.

380. From these imperfect hints it would appear, That every breach of Veracity indicates some latent vice, or some criminal intention, which an individual is ashamed to avow:—And hence the peculiar beauty of openness or sincerity,

---

* See Reid's Inquiry, chap. vi. sect. 24; and Smith's Theory, &c., last edit. vol. ii. p. 326.

uniting in some degree in itself the graces of all the other moral qualities of which it attests the existence.

381. Fidelity to promises, which is commonly regarded as a branch of Veracity, is perhaps more properly a branch of Justice: but this is merely a question of arrangement, and of little consequence to our present purpose.

382. If a person give his promise, intending to perform, but fails in the execution, his fault is, strictly speaking, a breach of Justice. As there is a natural faith in testimony, so there is a natural expectation excited by a promise. When I excite this expectation, and lead other men to act accordingly, I convey a right to the performance of my promise, and I act unjustly if I fail in performing it.

383. If a person promises,—not intending to perform, he is guilty of a complication of injustice and falsehood; for although a declaration of present intention does not amount to a promise, every promise involves a declaration of present intention.

384. In the cases which have been hitherto mentioned, the practice of Veracity is secured to a considerable extent in modern Europe by the received maxims of *Honour*, which brand with infamy every palpable deviation from the truth in matters of fact, or in the fulfilment of promises. Veracity, however, considered as a moral duty, is not confined to sincerity in the use of speech; but prohibits every circumstance in our external conduct which is calculated to mislead others, by conveying to them false information. It prohibits, in like manner, the wilful employment of sophistry in an argument, no less than a wilful misrepresentation of fact. The fashion of the times may establish distinctions in these different cases; but none of them are sanctioned by the principles of morality.

385. The same disposition of mind which leads to the practice of Veracity in our commerce with the world cherishes the love of Truth in our philosophical inquiries. This active principle (which is indeed but another name for the principle of Curiosity) seems also to be an ultimate fact in the human frame.

386. Although, however, in its first origin not resolvable into views of utility, the gradual discovery of its extensive effects on human improvement cannot fail to confirm and to

augment its native influence on the mind. The connection between error and misery, between truth and happiness, becomes more apparent as our researches proceed; producing at last a complete conviction, that even in those cases where we are unable to trace it the connection subsists; and encouraging the free and unbiassed exercise of our rational powers, as an expression, at once, of benevolence to man, and of confidence in the righteous administration of the universe.

387. The duties which have been mentioned in this article are all independent of any particular relation between us and other men. But there is a great variety of other duties resulting from such relations: The duties (for example) of Friendship and of Patriotism; besides those relative duties which moralists have distinguished by the titles of Economical and Political. To attempt an enumeration of these would lead into the details of practical Ethics.

SECTION III.

Of the Duties which respect Ourselves.

ARTICLE FIRST.

GENERAL REMARKS ON THIS CLASS OF OUR DUTIES.

388. Prudence, Temperance, and Fortitude, are no less requisite for enabling us to discharge our social duties than for securing our own private happiness: but as they do not necessarily imply any reference to our fellow-creatures, they seem to belong most properly to this third branch of Virtue.

389. An illustration of the nature and tendency of these qualities, and of the means by which they are to be improved and confirmed, although a most important article of Ethics, does not lead to any discussions of so abstract a kind as to require particular attention in a work of which brevity is a principal object.

390. It is sufficient here to remark that, independently of all considerations of utility, either to ourselves or to

others, these qualities are approved of as right and becoming. —Their utility, at the same time, or rather necessity, for securing the discharge of our other duties, adds greatly to the respect they command; and is certainly the chief ground of the obligation we lie under to cultivate the habits by which they are formed.

391. A steady regard, in the conduct of life, to the happiness and perfection of our own nature, and a diligent study of the means by which these ends may be attained, is another duty belonging to this branch of virtue. It is a duty so important and comprehensive that it leads to the practice of all the rest; and is therefore entitled to a very full and particular examination, in a system of Moral Philosophy. Such an examination, while it leads our thoughts "to the end and aim of our being," will again bring under our review the various duties already considered; and, by showing how they all conspire in recommending the same dispositions, will illustrate the unity of design in the human constitution, and the benevolent wisdom displayed in its formation. Other subordinate duties, besides, which it would be tedious to enumerate under separate titles, may thus be placed in a light more interesting and agreeable.

ARTICLE SECOND.

OF THE DUTY OF EMPLOYING THE MEANS WE POSSESS TO PROMOTE OUR OWN HAPPINESS.

392. According to Dr Hutcheson, our conduct, so far as it is influenced by self-love, is never the object of moral approbation. Even a regard to the pleasures of a good conscience he considered as detracting from the merit of those actions which it encourages us to perform.

393. That the principle of Self-love (or, in other words, the desire of happiness) is neither an object of approbation nor of blame, is sufficiently obvious. It is inseparable from the nature of man as a rational and a sensitive being (§ 161.).

394. It is however no less obvious, on the other hand, that this desire, considered as a principle of action, has by no means a uniform influence on the conduct. Our animal

appetites, our affections, and the other inferior principles of our nature, interfere as often with self-love as with benevolence, and mislead us from our own happiness as much as from the duties we owe to others.

395. In these cases every spectator pronounces that we *deserve* to suffer for our folly and indiscretion; and we ourselves, as soon as the tumult of passion is over, feel in the same manner. Nor is this remorse merely a sentiment of regret for having missed that happiness which we might have enjoyed. We are dissatisfied, not with our condition merely, but with our conduct—with our having forfeited, by our own imprudence, what we might have attained.*

396. It is true that we do not feel so warm an indignation against the neglect of private good, as against perfidy, cruelty, and injustice: the reason probably is, that imprudence commonly carries its own punishment along with it; and our resentment is disarmed by pity.—Indeed, as that habitual regard to his own happiness which every man feels, unless when under the influence of some violent appetite, is a powerful check on imprudence, it was less necessary to provide an additional punishment for this vice in the indignation of the world.

397. From the principles now stated it follows that, in a person who believes in a future state, the criminality of every bad action is aggravated by the imprudence with which it is accompanied.

398. It follows, also, that the punishments annexed by the civil magistrate to particular actions, render the commission of them more criminal than it would otherwise be;—insomuch, that if an action, in itself perfectly indifferent, were prohibited by some arbitrary law, under a severe penalty, the commission of that action (unless we were called to it by some urgent consideration of duty) would be criminal not merely on account of the obedience which a subject owes to established authority, but on account of the regard which every man ought to feel for his life and reputation.

* See Butler's Dissertation on the Nature of Virtue.

ARTICLE THIRD.

OF HAPPINESS.

399. The most superficial observation of life is sufficient to convince us that happiness is not to be attained by giving every appetite and desire the gratification they demand; and that it is necessary for us to form to ourselves some plan or system of conduct, in subordination to which all other objects are to be pursued.

400. To ascertain what this system ought to be is a problem which has in all ages employed the speculations of philosophers. Among the ancients it was the principal subject of controversy which divided the schools; and it was treated in such a manner as to involve almost every other question of Ethics. The opinions maintained with respect to it by some of their sects comprehended many of the most important truths to which the inquiry leads; and leave little to be added but a few corrections and limitations of their conclusions.

I. *Opinions of the Ancients concerning the Sovereign Good.**

401. These opinions may be all reduced to three; those of the Epicureans, of the Stoics, and of the Peripatetics.

402. According to Epicurus, bodily pleasure and pain are the sole ultimate objects of desire and aversion; and everything else is desired or shunned, from its supposed tendency to procure the former or to save us from the latter. Even the virtues are not valuable on their own account, but as the means of subjecting our pleasures and pains to our own power.†

403. The pleasures and pains of the mind are all derived (in the system of this Philosopher) from the recollection and anticipation of those of the body: but these recollections and anticipations are represented as of more value to our happiness, on the whole, than the pleasures and pains from which they are derived; for they occupy a much greater

---

* See Institutes of Moral Philosophy, by Dr Ferguson.
† Cicero de Finibus, i. 13.

proportion of life, and the regulation of them depends on ourselves. Epicurus, therefore, placed the supreme good in ease of body and tranquillity of mind, but much more in the latter than in the former;—insomuch that he affirmed that a wise man might preserve his happiness under any degree of bodily suffering.

404. Notwithstanding the errors and paradoxes of this system, and the very dangerous language in which its principles are expressed, it deserves the attention of those who prosecute moral inquiries on account of the testimony it bears to the connection between Virtue and Happiness. And accordingly Mr Smith remarks that, "Seneca, though a Stoic, the sect most opposite to that of Epicurus, yet quotes this philosopher more frequently than any other."

405. The Stoics placed the supreme good in rectitude of conduct, without any regard to the event.

406. They did not, however, recommend an indifference to external objects, or a life of inactivity and apathy; but, on the contrary, they taught that Nature pointed out to us certain objects of choice and rejection, and amongst these some as more to be chosen and avoided than others; and that virtue consisted in choosing and rejecting objects according to their intrinsic value. They only contended, that these objects should be pursued, not as the means of our happiness, but because we believe it to be agreeable to nature that we should pursue them; and that, therefore, when we have done our utmost, we should regard the event as indifferent.

407. The scale of desirable objects exhibited in this system was peculiarly calculated to encourage the social virtues. It taught that the prosperity of two was preferable to that of one: that of a city to that of a family; and that of our country to all partial considerations.—On this principle, added to a sublime sentiment of piety, it founded its chief argument for an entire resignation to the dispensations of Providence. As all events are ordered by perfect wisdom and goodness, the Stoics concluded, that whatever happens is calculated to produce the greatest possible good to the universe in general. As it is agreeable, therefore, to Nature that we should prefer the happiness of many to that of a few, and of all to that of many, they concluded that every event which happens, is precisely that which we

ourselves would have desired, if we had been acquainted with the whole scheme of the Divine administration.

408. While the Stoics held this elevated language, they acknowledged the weaknesses of humanity; but insisted that it is the business of the philosopher to delineate what is perfect, without lowering the dignity of Virtue by limitations arising from the frailties of mankind.*

409. In the greater part of these opinions the Peripatetics agreed with the Stoics. They admitted that Virtue ought to be the law of our conduct, and that no other good was to be compared to it; but they did not represent it as the *sole* good, nor affect a total indifference to things external. "Pugnant Stoici cum Peripateticis (says Cicero): Alteri negant quidquam bonum esse nisi quod honestum sit; alteri longe longeque plurimum se attribuere honestati; sed tamen et in corpore et extra esse quædam bona.—Certamen honestum, et disputatio splendida."

410. On the whole it appears (to use the words of Dr. Ferguson) that "all these sects acknowledged the necessity of virtue; or allowed that in every well-directed pursuit of happiness the strictest regard to morality was required. The Stoics alone maintained that this regard itself was happiness, or that to run the course of an active, strenuous, wise, and beneficent mind, was itself the very good which we ought to pursue."

II. *Additional Remarks on Happiness.*

411. From the slight view now given of the systems of philosophers, with respect to the sovereign good, it may be assumed as an acknowledged and indisputable fact, that happiness arises chiefly from the Mind. The Stoics perhaps expressed this too strongly, when they said that to a wise man external circumstances are indifferent. Yet it must be confessed that happiness depends much less on these than is

* The most important doctrines of this school have been illustrated by Dr Ferguson, with that depth and eloquence which distinguish all his writings, in a work lately published on the Principles of Moral and Political Philosophy.

The reader may also consult the Account of the Stoical System in Mr Smith's Theory, last edition; and the notes subjoined by Mr Harris to his Dialogue on Happiness.

commonly imagined; and that as there is no situation so prosperous as to exclude the torments of malice, cowardice, and remorse; so there is none so adverse as to withhold the enjoyments of a benevolent, resolute, and upright heart.

412. If from the sublime idea of a perfectly wise and virtuous man we descend to such characters as the world presents to us, some important limitations of the Stoical conclusions become necessary. Mr Hume has remarked, that " as in the bodily system a *toothache* produces more violent convulsions of pain than a *phthisis* or a *dropsy;* so in the economy of the mind, although all vice be pernicious, yet the disturbance or pain is not measured out by nature with exact proportion to the degree of vice."—The same author adds, that " if a man be liable to a vice or imperfection, it may often happen that a good quality which he possesses along with it will render him more miserable than if he were completely vicious."

413. Abstracting even from these considerations, and supposing a character as perfect as the frailty of human nature admits of, various mental qualities, which have no immediate connection with moral desert, are necessary to insure happiness. In proof of this remark it is sufficient to consider how much our tranquillity is liable to be affected,

(1.) By our temper.
(2.) By our imagination.
(3.) By our opinions. And,
(4.) By our habits.

414. In all these respects the mind may be influenced to a great degree by original constitution, or by early education; and when this influence happens to be unfavourable it is not to be corrected at once by the precepts of philosophy. Much, however, may undoubtedly be done, in such instances, by our own persevering efforts; and therefore the particulars now enumerated deserve our attention, not only from their connection with the speculative question, concerning the essentials of happiness, but on account of the practical conclusions to which the consideration of them may lead.

Influence of the Temper on Happiness.

415. The word Temper, which has various significations

in our language, is here used to express the habitual state of the mind in point of Irascibility,—a part of the character intimately connected with happiness, in consequence of the pleasures and pains attached respectively to the exercise of our benevolent and malevolent affections (§ 147, 157.).

416. Resentment was distinguished (§ 154.) into Instinctive and Deliberate; the latter of which, it was observed (§ 105.), has always a reference to the motives of the person against whom it is directed, and implies a sense of justice, or of moral good and evil.

417. In some men the animal or instinctive impulse is stronger than in others. Where this is the case, or where proper care has not been taken in early education to bring it under restraint, a quick or irascible temper is the necessary consequence. It is a fault frequently observable in affectionate and generous characters, and impairs their happiness, not so much by the effects it produces on their minds, as by the eventual misfortunes to which it exposes them.

418. When the animal resentment does not immediately subside it must be supported by an opinion of bad intention in its object; and, consequently, when this happens to an individual so habitually as to be characteristical of his temper, it indicates a disposition on his part to put unfavourable constructions on the actions of others. In some instances this may proceed from a settled conviction of the worthlessness of mankind; but in general it originates in self-dissatisfaction, occasioned by the consciousness of vice or folly, which leads the person who feels it to withdraw his attention from himself, by referring the causes of his ill-humour to the imaginary faults of his neighbours.

419. For curing these mental disorders, nothing is so effectual as the cultivation of that candour with respect to the motives of others which results from habits of attention to our own infirmities, and to the numerous circumstances which, independently of any criminal intention, produce the appearance of vice in human conduct (§ 360.).

420. By suppressing, too, as far as possible, the external signs of peevishness or of violence, much may be done to produce a gradual alteration in the state of the mind, and to render us not only more agreeable to others, but more

happy in ourselves.—So intimate is the connection between mind and body, that the mere imitation of any strong expression has a tendency to excite the corresponding passion; and, on the other hand, the suppression of the external sign has a tendency to compose the passion which it indicates.

421. The influence of the temper on happiness is much increased by another circumstance. That the same causes which alienate our hearts from our fellow-creatures are apt to suggest unfavourable views of the course of human affairs; and lead, by an easy transition, to a desponding scepticism.

422. As the temper has, in these instances, an influence on the opinions, so the views we form of the administration of the universe, and in particular of the condition and prospects of man, have a reciprocal influence on the temper. The belief of overruling wisdom and goodness communicates the most heartfelt of all satisfactions; and the idea of prevailing order and happiness has an habitual effect in composing the discordant affections, similar to what we experience, when in some retired and tranquil scene we enjoy the sweet serenity of a summer evening.

Influence of the Imagination on Happiness.

423. One of the principal effects of a liberal education is to accustom us to withdraw our attention from the objects of our present perceptions, and to dwell at pleasure on the past, the absent, and the future. How much it must enlarge in this way the sphere of our enjoyment or suffering is obvious; for (not to mention the recollection of the past) all that part of our happiness or misery which arises from our hopes or our fears derives its existence entirely from the power of Imagination.

424. In some men, indeed, imagination produces little either of pleasure or of pain; its exercise being limited, in a great measure, to the anticipation or recollection of sensual gratifications.

425. To others it is an instrument of exquisite distress;—where the mind, for instance, has been early depressed with scepticism, or alarmed with the terrors of superstition.

426. To those whose education has been fortunately con-

ducted, it opens inexhaustible sources of delight, presenting continually to their thoughts the fairest views of mankind and of Providence ; and, under the deepest gloom of adverse fortune, gilding the prospects of futurity.

427. The liveliness of the pictures which imagination exhibits depends probably, in part, on original constitution ; but much more on the care with which this faculty has been cultivated in our tender years. The complexion of these pictures, in point of gaiety or sadness, depends almost entirely on the associations which our first habits have led us to form.

428. Even on those men whose imaginations have received little or no cultivation, the influence of association is great ; and enters more or less into every estimate they form of the value of external objects. Much may be done by a wise education to render this part of our constitution subservient to our happiness (§ 60.).

429. Where the mind has been hurt by early impressions, they are not to be corrected wholly by Reasoning. More is to be expected from the opposite associations, which may be gradually formed by a new course of studies and of occupations, or by a complete change of scenes, of habits, and of society.

Influence of Opinions on Happiness.

430. By Opinions are here meant, not merely speculative conclusions to which we have given our assent, but convictions which have taken root in the mind, and have an habitual influence on the conduct.

431. Of these opinions a very great and important part are, in the case of all mankind, interwoven by education with their first habits of thinking, or are insensibly imbibed from the manners of the times.

432. Where such opinions are erroneous, they may often be corrected, to a great degree, by the persevering efforts of a reflecting and a vigorous mind ; but as the number of minds capable of reflection is comparatively small, it becomes a duty on all who have themselves experienced the happy effects of juster and more elevated principles, to impart as far as they are able the same blessing to others.—

The subject is of too great extent to be prosecuted in a treatise of which the plan excludes all attempts at illustration, but the reader will find it discussed at great length in a very valuable section of Dr Ferguson's Principles of Moral and Political Science.*

Influence of Habits on Happiness.

433. The effects of Habit in reconciling our minds to the inconveniencies of our situation was formerly remarked (§ 314.): and an argument was drawn from it in proof of the goodness of our Creator, who, beside making so rich a provision of objects suited to the principles of our nature, has thus bestowed on us a power of accommodation to external circumstances which these principles teach us to avoid.

434. This tendency, however, of the mind to adapt itself to the objects with which it is familiarly conversant, may, in some instances, not only be a source of occasional suffering, but may disqualify us for relishing the best enjoyments which human life affords. The habits contracted during infancy and childhood are so much more inveterate than those of our maturer years, that they have been justly said to constitute a second nature; and if unfortunately they have been formed amidst circumstances over which we have no control, they leave us no security for our happiness but the caprice of fortune.

435. To habituate the minds of children to those occupations and enjoyments alone which it is in the power of an individual at all times to command is the most solid foundation that can be laid for their future tranquillity. These too are the occupations and enjoyments which afford the most genuine and substantial satisfaction, and if education were judiciously employed to second in this respect the recommendations of nature, they might appropriate to themselves all the borrowed charms which the vanities of the world derive from casual associations.

436. With respect to pursuits which depend in the first instance on our own choice, it is of the last consequence for

* Part II. chap. i. sect. 8.

us to keep constantly in view how much of the happiness of mankind arises from habit, and in the formation of our plans to disregard those prepossessions and prejudices which so often warp the judgment in the conduct of life. "Choose that course of action (says Pythagoras) which is best, and custom will soon render it the most agreeable."

437. The foregoing remarks relate to what may be called the essentials of happiness;—the circumstances which constitute the general state or habit of mind that is necessary to lay a groundwork for every other enjoyment.

438. This foundation being supposed, the sum of happiness enjoyed by an individual will be proportioned to the degree in which he is able to secure all the various pleasures belonging to our nature.

439. These pleasures may be referred to the following heads.

(1.) The pleasures of Activity and Repose.
(2.) The pleasures of Sense.
(3.) The pleasures of Imagination.
(4.) The pleasures of the Understanding.
(5.) The pleasures of the Heart.

440. An examination and comparison of these different classes of our enjoyments is necessary, even on the Stoical principles, to complete the inquiry concerning happiness; in order to ascertain the relative value of the different objects of choice and rejection.

441. Such an examination, however, would lead into details inconsistent with the plan, and foreign to the design, of these outlines.—To those who choose to prosecute the subject, it opens a field of speculation equally curious and useful, and much less exhausted by moralists than might have been expected from its importance.

442. The practical conclusion resulting from the inquiry is, That the wisest plan of economy, with respect to our pleasures, is not merely compatible with a strict observance of the rules of morality, but is, in a great measure, comprehended in these rules; and, therefore, that the happiness, as well as the perfection of our nature, consists in

doing our duty, with as little solicitude about the event as is consistent with the weakness of humanity.

443. It may be useful once more to remark (§ 172. (3.), before leaving the subject, That notwithstanding these happy effects of a virtuous life, the principles of Duty and the desire of Happiness are radically distinct from each other. The peace of mind, indeed, which is the immediate reward of good actions, and the sense of merit with which they are accompanied, create, independently of experience, a very strong presumption in favour of the connection between Happiness and Virtue; but the facts in human life which justify this conclusion are not obvious to careless spectators; nor would philosophers in every age have agreed so unanimously in adopting it if they had not been led to the truth by a shorter and more direct process than an examination of the remote consequences of virtuous and of vicious conduct.

444. To this observation it may be added that, if the desire of Happiness were the sole, or even the ruling, principle of action in a good man, it could scarcely fail to frustrate its own object by filling his mind with anxious conjectures about futurity, and with perplexing calculations of the various chances of good and evil. Whereas, he whose ruling principle of action is a Sense of Duty, conducts himself in the business of life with boldness, consistency, and dignity, and finds himself rewarded by that Happiness which so often eludes the pursuit of those who exert every faculty of the mind in order to attain it.

SECTION IV.

Of the different Theories which have been formed concerning the Object of Moral Approbation.

445. It was before remarked (§ 245.), that the different Theories of Virtue which have prevailed in modern times have arisen chiefly from attempts to trace all the branches of our duty to one principle of action: such as a rational Self-love, Benevolence, Justice, or a disposition to obey the will of God.

446. That none of these Theories is agreeable to fact may be collected from the reasonings which have been already

stated. The harmony, however, which exists among our various good dispositions, and their general coincidence in determining us to the same course of life, bestows on all of them, when skilfully proposed, a certain degree of plausibility.

447. The systematical spirit from which they have taken their rise, although a fertile source of error, has not been without its use; inasmuch as it has roused the attention of ingenious men to the most important of all studies, that of the end and destination of human life. The facility, at the same time, with which so great a variety of consequences may be all traced from distinct principles, affords a demonstration of that unity and consistency of design which is no less conspicuous in the moral than in the material world.

SECTION V.

Of the General Definition of Virtue.

448. The various duties which have now been considered all agree with each other in one common quality, that of being *obligatory* on rational and voluntary agents; and they are all enjoined by the same authority,—the authority of conscience. These duties, therefore, are but different articles of one law, which is properly expressed by the word Virtue.

449. The same word (as will be more particularly stated in the next Section) is employed to express the moral excellence of a character. When so employed, it seems properly to denote a confirmed Habit of mind, as distinguished from good dispositions operating occasionally. It was formerly said (§ 161.), that the characters of men receive their denominations of Covetous, Voluptuous, Ambitious, &c., from the particular active principle which prevailingly influences the conduct. A man, accordingly, whose ruling or habitual principle of action is a sense of Duty, or a regard to what is Right, may be properly denominated Virtuous.— Agreeably to this view of the subject, the ancient Pythagoreans defined Virtue to be ‘Εξις του δεοντος:—the oldest definition of Virtue of which we have any account, and the most unexceptionable, perhaps, which is yet to be found in any system of philosophy.

450. These observations lead to an explanation of what

has at first sight the appearance of paradox in the ethical doctrines of Aristotle: that where there is Self-denial there is no Virtue.* That the merit of particular actions is increased by the self-denial with which they are accompanied cannot be disputed: but it is only when we are learning the practice of our duties that this self-denial is exercised (for the practice of morality, as well as of everything else, is facilitated by repeated acts); and, therefore, if the word Virtue be employed to express that habit of mind which it is the great object of a good man to confirm, it will follow that, in proportion as he approaches to it, his efforts of self-denial must diminish; and that all occasion for them would cease if his end were completely attained.

SECTION VI.

Of an Ambiguity in the words Right and Wrong, Virtue and Vice.

451. The epithets Right and Wrong, Virtuous and Vicious, are applied sometimes to external actions, and sometimes to the intentions of the Agent. A similar ambiguity may be remarked in the corresponding words in other languages.

452. The distinction made by some moralists between Absolute and Relative Rectitude was introduced in order to obviate the confusion of ideas which this ambiguity has a tendency to produce; and it is a distinction of so great importance as to merit a particular illustration in a system of Ethics.

453. An action may be said to be Absolutely right when it is in every respect suitable to the circumstances in which the agent is placed: or, in other words, when it is such as, with perfectly good intentions, under the guidance of an enlightened and well-informed understanding, he would have performed.

454. An action may be said to be Relatively right when the intentions of the agent are sincerely good;—whether his conduct be suitable to his circumstances or not.

455. According to these definitions, an action may be right in one sense and wrong in another:—An ambiguity

* Ancient Metaphysics, vol. iii. p. 12 of the Preface.

in language, which, how obvious soever, has not always been attended to by the writers on morals.

456. It is the relative rectitude of an action which determines the moral desert of the agent; but it is its absolute rectitude which determines its utility to his worldly interests, and to the welfare of society.—And it is only so far as relative and absolute rectitude coincide that utility can be affirmed to be a quality of virtue.

457. A strong sense of duty will indeed induce us to avail ourselves of all the talents we possess, and of all the information within our reach, to act agreeably to the rules of absolute rectitude. And if we fail in doing so, our negligence is criminal. But still, in every particular instance, our duty consists in doing what appears to us to be right at the time; and if, while we follow this rule, we should incur any blame, our demerit does not arise from acting according to an erroneous judgment, but from our previous misemployment of the means we possessed for correcting the errors to which our judgment is liable.

458. From these principles it follows, That actions, although materially right, are not meritorious with respect to the agent, unless performed from a sense of duty. This sense necessarily accompanies every action which is an object of moral approbation.

SECTION VII.

Of the Office and Use of Reason in the Practice of Morality.

459. It was observed (§ 457.), that a strong sense of duty, while it leads us to cultivate with care our good dispositions, will induce us to avail ourselves of all the means in our power for the wise regulation of our external conduct. The occasions on which it is necessary for us to employ our reason in this way are chiefly the three following.

(1.) When we have ground for suspecting that our moral judgments and feelings may have been warped and perverted by the prejudices of education.

(2.) When there appears to be an interference between different duties so as to render it doubtful in what the exact propriety of conduct consists.—To this head may be referred those cases in which the rights of different parties are concerned.

(3.) When the ends at which our duty prompts us to aim are to be accomplished by means which require choice and deliberation.

460. It is owing to the last of these considerations that the study of happiness, both private and public, becomes an important part of the science of Ethics. Indeed, without this study the best dispositions of the heart, whether relating to ourselves or to others, may be in a great measure useless.

461. The subject of happiness, so far as relates to the individual, has been already considered. The great extent and difficulty of those inquiries which have for their object to ascertain what constitutes the happiness of a community, and by what means it may be most effectually promoted, make it necessary to separate them from the other questions of Ethics, and to form them into a distinct branch of the science.

462. It is not, however, in this respect alone, that politics are connected with the other branches of Moral Philosophy. The provisions which nature has made for the intellectual and moral progress of the species all suppose the existence of the political union; and the particular form which this union happens in the case of any community to assume, determines many of the most important circumstances in the character of the people, and many of those opinions and habits which affect the happiness of private life.

APPENDIX.

PART III.

OF MAN CONSIDERED AS THE MEMBER OF A POLITICAL BODY.*

CHAPTER I.

OF THE HISTORY OF POLITICAL SOCIETY.

ARTICLE I.

Of the Principles in Human Nature, and of the Circumstances in the Condition of Mankind, which lay the Foundation of the Political Union.

ARTICLE II.

Of the Principles and Circumstances which lay the Foundation of the Progress of Society.

ARTICLE III.

Of the Institution of Marriage; and its Consequences, Political and Moral.

ARTICLE IV.

Of the Condition and the Character of the Sexes, as they are modified by different States of Society.

* See Preface.

ARTICLE V.

Of the History of Property, considered in relation to Human Improvement and Happiness.

ARTICLE VI.

Of the Origin and Progress of the Arts and the Sciences.

ARTICLE VII.

Of the Origin and Progress of Commerce.

ARTICLE VIII.

Of the Origin and Progress of Government, Rank, and Subordination.

ARTICLE IX.

Of the Origin and Progress of Municipal Systems of Jurisprudence.

ARTICLE X.

Of Diversities in the History of the Species, arising from the influence of Climate and Situation.

CHAPTER II.

OF THE GENERAL PRINCIPLES OF LEGISLATION AND GOVERNMENT.

SECTION I.

Of Political Economy.

ARTICLE I.

Of the Writings of *Grotius* and his Successors on Natural Jurisprudence, and their influence in suggesting the Modern Speculations concerning Political Economy.

ARTICLE II.

Of the Objects of Political Economy, and the more important general Conclusions to which the Study of it has led.

ARTICLE III.

Of the Coincidence of the Principles of Justice and of Expediency in the Political Conclusions to which they lead.

ARTICLE IV.

Of the Connection between just Views of Political Economy, and the Intellectual and Moral Improvement of Mankind.

SECTION II.

Of the different Functions of Government; and of the various Forms in which they are combined in the constitutions of different States.

ARTICLE I.

Of the Legislative, Judicial, and Executive Powers.

ARTICLE II.

Of the Simple Forms of Government, according to the definitions of speculative Politicians; and of the Uses to which this theoretical view of the subject is subservient in the examination of actual Constitutions.

ARTICLE III.

Of Mixed Governments.

ARTICLE IV.

Of the English Constitution.

ARTICLE V.

Of the Influence of Forms of Government on National Character and Manners.

ARTICLE VI.

Of the Duties arising from the Political Union.

ARTICLE VII.

Of the Political Relations of different States to each other, and of the Laws of Morality as applicable to Nations.

SUPPLEMENT.

ART. I.—THE METHOD OF INQUIRY. Introduction, pp. 1—4.

The Method of Inquiry recommended in the text is that of Induction with Self-Consciousness as the agent of observation. It should be understood, however, (1) that we may acquire knowledge of the operations of the mind, not only by immediate inspection of the present mental state, and by the memory as we recall the past, but also and more specially by what we discover of other men's thoughts and feelings as expressed in their words, their writings, and their actions, which we can understand and appreciate because of its resemblance to what we feel in ourselves. Then (2) conjoined with Induction there must commonly be Deduction. Supposing that the law is of such a nature, that is, devising an Hypothesis, we inquire whether the facts correspond; when they so far do so we have a Theory, which when established by an extensive induction may become a Law of Nature. This process of comparing with facts the results reached by deduction is called Verification of Inductions. In this Joint Method of Induction and Deduction care must be taken that the Hypothesis arise out of the facts observed, and be not a mere creation of the fancy; and that it be sedulously verified by facts, and rejected if it cannot stand the test. In the process of scientific observation, Analysis (mental), or what Whewell calls the Decomposition of Facts, which facts are always concrete or complex, is an essential element. Synthesis seems rather a scientific mode of teaching science,—that is, supposing the law to have been discovered, we unfold the parts and show that they make up the whole.

ART. II.—MORAL PHILOSOPHY. p. 5, § 1.

As Logic is now very commonly defined the Science of the Laws of Thought (that is, Discursive Thought), so Moral Philosophy or Ethics may be regarded as the Science of the Laws of Man's Moral Constitution, embracing the Conscience and the Will, looking to the other powers, such as the understanding and the emotions, so far as they are capable of being swayed by these, and to outward circumstances, as it is in them that man's moral nature acts. This science may be described as *a priori*, inasmuch as the laws of man's constitution are in his nature prior to and independent of experience; but it is *a posteriori*, inasmuch as they operate only where experience calls them forth, and they can be discovered by us and scientifically expressed only by a careful observation of their actual workings.

PART I.

ART. III.—SELF-CONSCIOUSNESS. p. 7, § 7—11.

The Author does not seem to have unfolded all that is in self-consciousness. We are conscious, not certainly of mind apart from its operations, but just as little of the operations apart from mind. We are conscious of both in one concrete act; we are conscious of self operating. We are not conscious "of our own existence" apart from our existence in a particular state, but we are conscious of ourselves as existing in a particular state. Of the present operations of the mind consciousness is always a part, rather than a "concomitant." It is only by taking this view that we can successfully meet the scepticism of Hume, or the subtler scepticism of Kant, who represents us as conscious only of the *phenomena* (appearances) or manifestations of mind, whereas we are conscious of self as a thing or existence manifesting itself. Being thus conscious of self our conviction of our personal identity is a conviction of a personal self—we are the same to-day as we were yesterday.

ART. IV.—THE MUSCULAR SENSE. pp. 7, 8, § 12, 13, 18, 21.

The sense of Touch vulgarly understood is now divided into two senses, Touch Proper or Feeling, and the Muscular Sense embracing the Locomotive Energy. In Touch Proper we perceive merely an affection of the bodily frame. By the Muscular Sense we perceive an object external to the body and affecting it, and resisting our voluntary energy in moving the body. The physiological apparatus of this latter consists of an *efferent* Motor Nerve going out from the brain and reaching a muscle; and of an *afferent* Sensor Nerve going back to the seat of sensation in the brain. We will to move a particular part of the body, and there is an action from the brain along the efferent nerve, and the muscle is moved—this is the Locomotive Energy; when this motion is resisted we are apprized of it by the sensor nerve.

ART. V.—THE OBJECT INTUITIVELY PERCEIVED BY THE VARIOUS SENSES. pp. 7—10, § 12—26.

In the case of the lower and more animal senses of Smell, Taste, Touch Proper, and Hearing all that we perceive intuitively is our body as affected in a particular manner. This, however, seems to imply, (1) that the body is different from the perceiving mind, that is, extra-mental; (2) that the parts perceived as they are out of the mind so they are also out of each other; and hence (3) a knowledge of extension, that is, of our body as extended. By the Muscular

Sense we seem to know the resisting object (see Art. iv.) not only as *extra-mental* but *extra-organic*, that is, we know not merely our bodily frame but an external object affecting it. Not only so, the voluntary effort in the Locomotive Energy gives us the knowledge of Power in self; and the resistance offered of Force in the extra-organic object. By Sight we seem to know a *coloured surface* in a relation to our felt and localized visual organ. This seems to be our *original* or *intuitive* stock of perceptions; all beyond is *acquired* by a gathered observation and a simple process of reasoning aided by the association of ideas (see § 60). Our intuitive perceptions are all of our sentient frame, or of objects immediately affecting it. It cannot be said then of any of the senses that "the object perceived is at a distance" (§ 13). *So far* there is truth in the Aristotelian doctrine, derived from Democritus, that all our senses are modifications of feeling (§ 12).

ART. VI.—QUALITIES OF MATTER. pp. 8—12, § 15, 19, 26, 31—33.

The Qualities of Matter, according to Locke, are of three sorts, the primary, the secondary, and those by which one body acts upon another (*Essay*, b. ii., c. 8, § 8—26). Sir W. Hamilton divides them into: (1.) The Primary, which are all evolved from two catholic conditions of matter, the occupying of space, and the being contained in space; and embrace Extension, Divisibility, Size, Density or Rarity, Figure, Incompressibility absolute, Mobility, Situation. (2.) The Secundo-Primary, which have a relation to space and motion in space, and are all contained under the category of resistance or pressure, and are three in number, Co-attraction, Repulsion, Inertia. (3.) The Secondary, which belong to bodies only so far as they are thought to be capable of specifically determining the various parts of our nervous apparatus (*Hamilton's Reid*, Note D.). These classifications are valuable mainly for metaphysical purposes, and are at best to be regarded as provisional. Physical and physiological science must advance several stages, and tell us more of the correlation of forces, of polar action, of cnemical affinity, of heat, electricity, and colour, before we can have an adequate arrangement of the properties of matter. The above classifications are all defective in this respect, that they omit, or at least do not explicitly include, power, active property, force, dynamical energy. We know matter in our primary cogitations as extended, but we also know it as exercising property. We cannot know our own bodies, or bodies out of it, except as operating, exercising property, that is, power (see Art. v).

ART. VII.—OUR IDEAS OF THE PRIMARY QUALITIES OF MATTER. pp. 8—13, § 15—19, 23, 26, 32.

According to Reid and Stewart, sensations are the signs which intuitively suggest the primary qualities of extension and figure. This account is unfortunate, as it implies that sensation is before perception, that the former *suggests* the latter, and that we immediately know only the sensation, and not the external thing. Sensation and perception come simultaneously and co-exist (*see Hamilton's Reid*, pp. 186, 883); and in perception we directly know the object as extended, we may add as exercising property. It should be added that intuitively we do not know extension or property in the abstract or general; we simply know the object in the concrete as extended, and as exercising property; and it is by a subsequent and discursive process that we separate in thought the space and the power from the extended acting object, and form the abstract or general idea of space and power.

ART. VIII.—THE VARIOUS FORMS OF THE IDEAL THEORY OF SENSE-PERCEPTION. pp. 12, 13, § 34—38.

According to Sir W. Hamilton (*Reid's Works, Note C. Discussions, Phil. of Per.*), philosophers are either Realists or Idealists. Realists are either Natural, who maintain that we know the external thing directly, or Hypothetical (= Cosmothetic Idealists), who suppose that there is a real world not directly known. Idealists are Absolute or Presentative, who suppose that there is only the idea; or Cosmothetic or Representative (= Hypothetical Realists), who hold that we know the external thing by a representation. The possible forms of the representative hypothesis are three: (1) The representative object not a modification of mind, but an extra-mental object physical or hyper-physical; (2) the representative object a modification of mind, dependent for its apprehension, but not for its existence, on the act of consciousness—say an idea in the mind, as was held apparently by Locke; (3) the representative object a modification of mind, non-existent out of consciousness, the idea and its perception only different relations of an act (state) really identical—the view taken by Arnauld and Brown.

ART. IX.—THE SEEMING DECEPTION OF THE SENSES.
pp. 11, § 29.   pp. 20, 21, § 71, 72.

It is of the utmost moment to show that the senses properly interpreted do not deceive; for if they lead us into error, other parts of our constitution may do the same. In order to preserve the veracity of the senses we must take along with us THREE DISTINCTIONS: I. The distinction between Sensation and Perception; the former being the mere subjective feeling, organic or psychical, the latter being the cognition of the extra-mental object by the mind. In our sense-perceptions we must distinguish between the object perceived, say the tooth, and the sensation attached, say the pain of toothache. II. The distinction between our Original and Acquired Perceptions (see § 23). Our Original Perceptions seem to be simply of our sentient body, or of objects immediately affecting it (see Art. v). These do not deceive us, at least when the mind is not deranged, and it is for these alone that our constitution, and the Author of our constitution are responsible. For our Acquired Perceptions we are ourselves responsible, and they may be right or wrong. In adding acquired to our original perceptions we form rules derived from experience; and we proceed on these, without reflection, simply by the laws of association. Now it may happen that these rules are correct for cases similar to those from which they were derived; but land us in mistakes when hurriedly applied by mere association to other cases. Thus we lay down the rule, that when we feel ourselves to be at rest, and an image of an object moves over the retina of the eye, this object is in motion. This rule is correct enough when we are on land; but in following it when we are in a ship sailing away from the shore it leads us to think that the quay is moving. But we are not to charge the error upon our intuitive perception, which is simply that of a coloured extended object in a certain relation to our localized visual organ (see Art. v.). In order to use this distinction properly we must attend, III. to the distinction between the Objects Intuitively Perceived. These are in some cases merely of our sentient body, and in other cases of extra-organic objects immediately affecting us. Thus smell, or hearing, cannot be said to deceive us as to extra-organic objects, for neither has any information to give in regard to such; and sight cannot deceive us as to distant objects, for it tells us only of a coloured surface in a particular relation to the optic organism.

ART. X.—THE RELATIVITY OF KNOWLEDGE. p. 11, § 28; p. 86, § 323.

By the two faculties of Sense-Perception and Self-Consciousness, we obtain knowledge; not, as is often said, impressions, ideas or notions, but *knowledge*, not abstract or scientific, but of singular objects in the concrete. In § 28, and 323, all our notions are represented as relative, whereas in § 31, our notions of the secondary qualities are represented as relative—as if those of the primary were something more. There is truth in the doctrine of Reid and Stewart that all knowledge is relative, but the phrase needs to be explained. The elaborate doctrine of the relativity of all knowledge drawn out by Sir W. Hamilton (*Discussions App.*) and proceeded on by Dr Mansel (*Bampton Lectures*), is not to be received without some very important explanations, cautions, and limitations. It should be admitted (1) that man knows objects only so far as he has faculties of knowledge; (2) that he knows objects only under the aspects presented to his faculties; and (3) that his faculties are limited, and consequently his knowledge limited, so that not only does he not know all objects, he does not know all about any one object. But, on the other hand, if we would defend the veracity of our faculties, and the reality of knowledge, it should be resolutely held, (1) that we know the very object or thing, and not a mere *phenomenon*, in the sense of appearance; and (2) that our knowledge is correct so far as it goes, and is not modified by the percipient mind. We admit a subtle scepticism when we allow, with Kant and Hamilton, that we do not know the thing itself, and that the mind adds to the object something not in it.

ART. XI.—UNCONSCIOUS MENTAL OPERATIONS. p. 14, § 41, 42.

Since the days of Leibnitz the question has often been discussed whether there are mental operations of which we are unconscious. The view of Stewart seems capable of being defended. It is a fact that there are many operations of which we are conscious at the time, but which are not capable of being recalled in ordinary circumstances. This fact seems to explain the whole phenomena, and we are not obliged to resort to an hypothesis which supposes a mode of operation of which we have no other evidence. According to Leibnitz and Hamilton the impression of the noise of the sea is made up of the impressions of the several waves, which impressions must be mental operations below consciousness. There is surely a misapprehension here. The intuitive perception is simply of an affection of the ear produced by undulations in the air, and not an impression of each wave (see Art. v.). The younger Fichte would account for the efforts of genius by unconscious action. They can be better explained by original endowment. It should be admitted that we are not conscious of mental powers or faculties, or acquired habits, but we seem to be always conscious at the moment of actual mental operations, though many of them are never recalled by the memory.

ART. XII. ABSTRACTION AND GENERALIZATION.
pp. 15, 16, § 47—52.

Stewart, like Locke, has not distinguished between Abstraction and Generalization. By sense-perception and self-consciousness we know objects as singulars and in the concrete, that is, we know single objects with an aggregate of qualities,—say this ball as extended and coloured. By Abstraction we contemplate a part of the concrete whole as a part, more specially a quality, of the object—say roundness, as a quality of the ball. In Generalization we contemplate objects as possessing the same quality or qualities. An abstract notion is the notion of a part as a part—specially of an attribute. A general notion is the notion of objects possessing a common attribute or common attributes; it embraces all the objects real or potential possessing the common attributes. These processes are registered and much aided by language; but in themselves they are mental processes. The language of Stewart and of Nominalists generally, as to the dependence of generalization and reasoning on language (§ 50. 89.), is too strong and unqualified.

ART. XIII.—ASSOCIATION OF IDEAS. pp. 16—18,
§ 53—60.

Aristotle thus arranges the associations of idea: διὸ καὶ τὸ ἐφεξῆς θηρεύομεν νοήσαντες ἀπὸ τοῦ νῦν ἢ ἄλλου τινός, καὶ ἀφ' ὁμοίου ἢ ἐναντίου ἢ τοῦ σύνεγγυς, in which he is commonly represented as making the laws those of Similarity, Contrast, and Contiguity (see another interpretation, *Hamilton's Reid, Note D* * * *). Some have endeavoured to reduce all the laws to one, commonly that of Contiguity (the Redintegration of Hamilton), that is, ideas that have co-existed in the mind, or followed each other, tend to recall each other. Stewart seems to be right in saying, that things related by any kind of relation tend to suggest each other. Besides these primary laws there are others called *secondary laws* by Brown (reduced to the Law of Preference by Hamilton), which incline us, among associated objects, to go after one rather than another. These laws may perhaps be reduced to two: to Original Taste or Disposition; and the Law of Energy, that is, the mind recalls most readily and frequently the ideas on which it has bestowed the greatest amount of Energy, and this, whether it be energy of intellect, of feeling, or of will.

ART. XIV.—COMPARISON, OR THE FACULTY OF RELATIONS. pp. 20—22, § 69, 70, 73—80.

In Judgment and Reasoning Stewart includes Intuition. But Intuition, or Intuitive Reason, is not a distinct faculty; it is involved in all our intellectual powers, for example, in Perception and Consciousness, as well as in Judgment. Stewart should here have introduced Comparison, or the Faculty which discovers various relations between objects known or apprehended (see Art. xvii.): and should under each of the faculties have unfolded the intuitions involved in them (see Art. xvi.).

ART. XV.—THE ARISTOTELIAN LOGIC. pp. 22, 23, § 77, 80.

The objections taken by Stewart to the Aristotelian analysis of reasoning have been answered by Whately (Elements of Logic). The conclusion does not follow from the major proposition, but from the major and minor combined. The natural process is thus:—This man | having taken laurel water | has taken poison |. When unfolded logically it becomes:—*Major premiss*, He who has drunk laurel water has drunk poison; *Minor premiss*, this man has drunk laurel water; *Conclusion*, he has drunk poison. The rule here is evidently the *Dictum* of Aristotle. There are disputes as to whether all reasoning falls under the *Dictum*. In cases where there is no general or class notion, the reasoning must fall under another rule.

ART. XVI.- INTUITION. pp. 20—22, § 70—77.

Stewart's threefold division of our Intuitions into (1) Axioms, (2) those of Self-Consciousness, Perception, and Memory, (3) Fundamental Laws of Belief, does not seem philosophical. They may be arranged :—I. PRIMITIVE COGNITIONS, in which, as in perception and consciousness, the object is now present. II. PRIMITIVE BELIEFS, in which we are convinced of the existence of objects not present, as of the continuity of space, time, and of infinity. III. PRIMITIVE JUDGMENTS, in which we perceive immediately the agreement or disagreement of two or more objects apprehended. It should be observed that these Intuitions, though naturally in the mind as regulative principles, always come forth into conscious operation as singulars or individuals, and can be known by us as general maxims or axioms only by a process of generalization—in which error may appear.

In the text the Tests of Intuition are not given. They seem to be, I. Self-evidence; the objects or truths are seen immediately, they shine in their own light. II. Necessity; we cannot be made in our primitive Cognitions, Beliefs, or Judgments, to know, believe, or judge otherwise. III. Catholicity; all men proceed on them.

ART. XVII.—CLASSIFICATION OF THE INTELLECTUAL POWERS. pp. 6, 23.

The following embraces all those enumerated by Stewart, with others which he has omitted.

I. SIMPLE COGNITIVE, OR PRESENTATIVE.
  1. Sense-Perception.
  2. Self-Consciousness.

II. REPRODUCTIVE, OR REPRESENTATIVE.
  1. Retentive.
  2. Associative.
  3. Imaging.
  4. Recognitive.
  5. Composition.
  6. Symbolic.

III. COMPARISON, OBSERVING RELATIONS OF
{
1. Identity.
2. Whole and Parts.
3. Resemblance.
4. Space.
5. Time.
6. Quantity.
7. Active Property.
8. Cause and Effect.
}

In explanation, it will be necessary only to say a few words on the Reproductive Powers. 1. The Retentive keeps in order to reproduce. 2. The reproduction takes place according to the Laws of Association. 3. The object comes into consciousness by an Image. 4. In memory it is Recognized as having been before the mind in time past (hence the idea of Time in the concrete). 5. In imagination it is put into new forms by Composition. 6. By the Symbolic Power it is thought by means of Signs, more especially Language. In Memory the powers involved are the Retentive, Associative, Imaging, and Recognitive Powers—the last being the essential element. In Imagination the powers are the Retentive, Associative, Imaging, and that of Composition—the last being the essential one.

PART II.

ART. XVIII.—DIVISION OF THE MENTAL FACULTIES.
p. 5, § 2, 3.   p. 30, § 110—112.

Instead of the twofold division of the Faculties of the Mind into those of the Understanding and Will, the more commonly-received arrangement in the present day is a threefold one, taken from Kant and adopted by Sir W. Hamilton, viz., 1. The Faculties of Knowledge. 2. The Feelings. 3. The Conative Powers, embracing Will and Desire. It may be objected to this division, first, that it must place among the Knowing Faculties the Imagination, which yet is cognizant of no object; and, secondly, it leaves out the Moral Faculty as a separate power, dividing it between the Cognitive and Conative Powers (see another division, Art.

xvii.). The powers called Active by Stewart, or, what seems a better nomenclature, Orective by Aristotle (Motive by Hobbes), are at least three in number, the Emotions (see Art. xix.), the Conscience (see Art. xx.), and the Will (see Art. xxi.).

ART. XIX.—SPRINGS OF ACTION AND EMOTIONS.
pp. 30—37, § 112—158.

Many good purposes might be served by a classification of the natural springs of appetence and action in the mind of man. Among them must be placed first the Appetence for Pleasure and the Aversion to Pain. But there are evidently a great many others, such as the Appetites and the mental Appetencies mentioned by Stewart, the Desires of Knowledge, of Society, of Esteem, of Power, of Superiority; and the disposition to seek the good of others, and the inclination toward beauty and moral good. The idea or apprehension of objects as fitted to gratify or disappoint these natural appetencies, or acquired ones founded on them, calls forth Emotions. One class, such as joy, hope, contemplate objects as appetible; others, such as grief and fear, contemplate objects as inappetible. The Emotions thus called forth are characterized by attachment or repugnance to the objects, together with excitement.

ART. XX.—DIFFERENT THEORIES OF THE NATURE OF THE MORAL FACULTY. pp. 44—58, § 171—222.

These may be classified as follows: 1. That which refers it to our personal feelings (the Selfish Theory), or social feelings, to one or both, aided by association of ideas, called forth by circumstances and man's social relations. This is the theory adopted by the utilitarians (see it examined Art. xxv.). 2. The Sentimental Theory, which ascribes it to a mere sense, sentiment, or feeling, as is done by Shaftesbury, Hutcheson, A. Smith, T. Brown, and Sir James Mackintosh (see this view noticed, § 188—195.). 3. The Rational Theory, which represents it as a power partaking of the nature of reason; this is done by Cudworth, Clarke, Price, and others (§ 196—199.). The Moral Power may be called a Sense, inasmuch as it is a cognitive power, discerning a peculiar quality, that is, a moral quality in certain actions. It can be shown that it is not a mere feeling or sentiment (§ 200.). The mind declares that honesty and piety are good, and cruelty and deceit evil, just as it declares that two parallel lines can never meet. On the other hand, whenever we apprehend (Art. xix.) a voluntary act as good, Emotion is excited.

ART. XXI.—THE WILL. pp. 63, 64, § 239—244.

The essential element of Will is *choice* or *rejection;* and so it is easily distinguished from Emotion (Art. xix.) and Conscience (Art. xx.). But under Will in this wide sense must be included, not only *Volition or the determination to act*, but also *Wish*. In Wish there is a voluntary exercise, we choose an object. In Will also are included our voluntary rejections. All virtuous acts must be voluntary; but in voluntary acts we must include Wishes as well as Volitions. "Whosoever looketh on a woman," &c., Matt. v. 28.

ART. XXII.—THE THEISTIC ARGUMENTS. pp. 65—78, § 248—285.

From the time of Aristotle to that of D. Hume, an argument *a priori* meant one from cause to effect, or from principle to consequent. In this sense S. Clarke's argument is *a priori*. Since the time of Hume and Kant, by an argument *a priori* is meant one drawn from internal principles independent of experience. In this sense Clarke's argument is not *a priori*, but *a posteriori*, for it proceeds upon an *experienced fact*, that we have an idea of space and time. The argument is that space and time, as they are not substances, must be modes of a being, who by other considerations is shown to be clothed with intelligence and moral perfections. But it is difficult to prove either *a priori* or *a posteriori*, that everything must be either a substance or a mode. Kant has a famous threefold arrangement of the theistic arguments. 1. The ONTOLOGICAL employed by Anselm, Descartes, and Leibnitz, and derived from the very idea of the infinite, the perfect, in the mind. This argument is *a priori*. But it may be denied that an idea, as an idea in the mind, implies the existence of a corresponding object—which can only be established by other considerations. 2. The COSMOLOGICAL, or that which argues from the world as a bare existence, to the existence of Absolute Being. This argument is *a posteriori* in the modern sense of the phrase, inasmuch as it supposes observed existence; it implies, however, the principle of cause and effect, which Kant declares to be *a priori*—but will not allow to imply any corresponding objective reality. It may be doubted whether a mere unformed mass of matter as an existence, would prove the existence of a cause, or of anything beyond itself. 3. The PHYSICO-THEOLOGICAL, or that from traces of design, or final cause. This argument is *a posteriori*, inasmuch as it proceeds on the obvious traces of adaptation in the universe (illustrations are furnished § 264—284.). But Kant has shown that it implies the *a priori* principle of causation. This argument is a valid one. We see traces in nature of effects; in particular, we see innumerable instances of adaptations working to a good end; and the internal principle of causation constrains us to rise to a belief of a cause in an intelligent and good Being. It has been far too readily allowed to Kant, not only by German, but of a late date by British theologians and metaphysicians, that he has overthrown this argument. Kant was precluded from acknowledging its validity, in consequence of his having adopted a defective and utterly erroneous view of causation, making it a mere form in the mind, and not a law of things. But our intuition of cause and effect, properly interpreted, insists that when the effect is a reality (objective) the cause must also be a reality. It can be farther shown that the intuition of cause and effect, while it requires us to seek for a cause of the traces of design in nature, does not require us to seek for an infinite series of causes (as Kant supposes), for all causation or power resides in a substance (see "Method of the Divine Government," Appendix, Art. I. IV.; and "Intuitions of the Mind," Part II. B. iii. c. i. § 8.). It should be added that the most potent and satisfactory argument for the Divine existence is that derived from man's moral nature, from the law in the heart implying a lawgiver.

ART. XXIII.—THE INFINITE. p. 78, § 285.

There has been a brilliant controversy in our day as to the Idea of the Infinite. Sir W. Hamilton (Art. "*Philosophy of the Unconditioned*," in "*Discussions*") and Dr Mansel (*Bampton Lectures*) argue, in opposition to Schelling and Cousin, that the *idea* is negative, while they allow that we have a *belief* in the Infinite. But surely a *belief* must imply some sort of *idea*, otherwise it would be a belief in nothing; indeed the arguments advanced against the idea tell equally against the belief. The question is, what sort of apprehension and conviction the mind has in regard to infinity. This is a question to be decided by an appeal to consciousness, and does not seem insoluble. In the idea and conviction which the mind intuitively entertains on this subject, two things seem implied:—*first*, the infinite object, say God, *is ever beyond our widest image or conception; secondly*, the infinite is such, that *nothing can be added to it*. Such an intuitive conviction is vastly less than is claimed by Schelling, or even by Cousin, but is vastly more than is allowed by Hamilton and Mansel. The idea is confessedly inadequate, but it is positive, and not simply negative. It is upon such an idea that our belief is fastened, and the two, the idea and belief, lead us to clothe God with the perfection of Infinity.

ART. XXIV.—MORAL EVIL. pp. 79—84, § 290—315.

The same Moral Faculty which gives its attestation to the reality and excellence of *moral good*, also testifies to the existence and evil of *sin*. It is curious to observe that Stewart, and other academic moralists, while they show so conclusively that man has a moral nature, take no notice of the fact that this nature condemns the possessor. Christian divines, appealing to man's conscious sinfulness, have argued that the Scripture doctrine of the atonement fits in beautifully to man's moral wants. The considerations advanced by Stewart (§ 290—315) show that the blame of moral evil may be thrown upon the agent who commits it, and that God brings good out of evil; but they by no means give a full explanation of the origin of moral evil, which is the great enigma of our universe, and perhaps the source of every other mystery

ART. XXV.—THE UTILITARIAN THEORY OF MORALS.
pp. 48—58, § 182—221. pp. 94—96, § 344—353.

Mr J. S. Mill has a plausible defence of this theory in his work on " Utilitarianism." But he has scarcely faced, and he has utterly failed to meet, the objections taken to the system.

I. He has not shown how we get the ideas involved in the words *ought, obligation, merit, demerit, sense of sin*. That man has such ideas, that, for example, he knows it to be wrong to tell a lie, is as certain as that he has the ideas of pleasure and pain—that he knows, for instance, that the taste of an apple is pleasant. The senses give us the latter idea. Whence do we receive the former? The idea of moral good cannot be had from the mere personal love of pleasure; this will never show that we *ought*, that we are *under an obligation*, to love our neighbour. Mr Mill seems to refer the idea to our social feelings (p. 45)—we are inclined to love our neighbour. Note here, that these *social feelings* are something higher than our *personal feelings*, and if man has *social feelings*, why may he not also have *moral affections*? We seem to have as conclusive proof, by the consciousness, of the existence of the one as of the other class of sentiments. But further, the mere social or sympathetic feelings cannot give the ideas, so very peculiar and so very profound, of moral approbation and disapprobation, desert, guilt. Mr Mill regards the "natural feeling of resentment" (p. 94) and the "idea of legal restraint," as " the generating idea of the notion of justice" (p. 71).

Stewart gives a more philosophical account (§ 155.): "Deliberate resentment is excited only by intentional injury, and therefore implies a sense of justice, or of moral good and evil."

II. According to Mr Mill and utilitarians, "happiness is desirable, and the only thing desirable, as an end" (p. 51). Every one will admit that happiness is a desirable end. Our consciousness reveals this. But the same consciousness declares that there are other desirable ends; not only so, but that there are higher ends. Mr M. allows that "it is better to be a human being dissatisfied, than a pig satisfied; better be a Socrates dissatisfied than a fool satisfied" (p. 14). This shows that there are other *qualities* sought and valued besides mere satisfaction, pleasure, or happiness. If we interpret our constitution aright, it declares that man may contemplate a higher end than the promotion of his own happiness, he may seek the furtherance of his own moral purity; he may have a higher end in view than the bestowing of enjoyments on others, he may aim at advancing their moral elevation.

III. Utilitarianism cannot show that man *ought* to promote the happiness of others. It fails at this point where it imagines itself to be strongest. "No reason," says Mr Mill, "can be given why the general happiness is desirable, except that each person, so far as he believes it to be attainable, desires his own happiness" (p. 52). But can this reason show that we are morally bound to promote the good of others? "The standard," says Mr M., very properly, "is not the agent's own happiness, but the greatest amount of happiness altogether;" "secured to all mankind, and not to them only, but, so far as the nature of things admits, to the whole sentient creation;" and again, "to do as you would be done by, and to love your neighbour as yourself, constitute the ideal perfection of utilitarian morality" (pp. 17, 24). It is a high ideal (though it wants its complement, "thou shalt love the Lord thy God with all thy heart"), but it is so high that utilitarianism cannot reach it. For where can utilitarianism get a sanction for all this? Why should I seek anything beyond my own happiness? Each man is led by certain natural appetencies to desire his own happiness, but why deny these, why ought I to deny these, in order to secure comforts for others?

There is a gap here which utilitarianism cannot fill up, except by help of a nobler system, which shows a moral power within us, pointing to a law and a lawgiver above us, requiring that we should love our neighbours as ourselves, but requiring, farther, that we should honour and obey God, and do what is right irrespective of consequences.

IV. Utilitarianism undermines the sanctions of morality. Mr M. indeed labours to show that it leaves these as it found them, and in particular that it does not interfere with those derived from public opinion, or those supposed to be given by religion. But by doing away with an independent moral obligation, it deprives public feeling of its moral support. Again, by discarding an eternal immutable law, it undermines the most irresistible of all the proofs for the existence of a God, and for the binding authority of religion. Further, by representing God as looking only to the enjoyment of his creatures, it takes away one of the most essential of the Divine Perfections, that of Holiness, or Justice. Mr M. argues dexterously, that in the last resort, the appeal of the independent morality school, as well as of the utilitarian school, is to *feeling, to "a feeling in our own mind"* (pp. 40, 41). Even on the supposition that this was the case, the feeling appealed to by the advocate of an eternal morality is different from that called in by the utilitarian. The latter can bring to his aid only a personal, or at best a sympathetic, feeling; the former appeals to a moral sentiment which claims to have a supremacy over all others. But the sanction and the standard of the opponents of utilitarianism is not mere feeling. It is not to subjective feeling we appeal when we say that things which are equal to the same thing are equal to one another; it is to the nature of things perceived by intuitive reason. Just as little is it to mere feeling that we appeal, when we affirm that love is good, that justice is good; it is to the reality of things disclosed by our moral perceptions.

ART. XXVI.—JUSTICE. p. 96, § 354.

The definition of Justice in the text seems to embrace only a particular manifestation of the virtue. That adopted by Justinian in the opening sentence of his Institutes is more correct and comprehensive: *Justitia est constans et perpetua voluntas jus suum cuique tribuendi.* It has a place wherever there are other beings besides ourselves. It implies an obligation, a moral obligation, to these beings, and a voluntary disposition (*voluntas*) or affection towards them. Veracity is a particular form or manifestation, so also is that disposition which throws off bias.

ART. XXVII.—BENEVOLENCE AS THE ULTIMATE END WITH DEITY. p. 95, § 348.

The language of the text is very guarded, but does not seem sanctioned by our constitution. "It is possible that in the Deity, benevolence or regard to utility may be the sole principle, and that the ultimate end for which he enjoined to his creatures the duties of veracity and justice was to secure their own happiness." Our moral nature clearly announces that there is a greater good than mere happiness, and that there may be a higher end than the promotion of happiness; there is, for example, the *love* that seeks to promote happiness, and the *justice* that guards and directs love. Our moral constitution declares that these last are good in themselves, and, if so, they must be good to God, who sees all things as they are. Stewart holds that when 1 say of an act of justice that it is right, "I mean to assert a truth which is as independent of my constitution as the equality of the three angles of a triangle to two right angles" (§ 200.). That the three angles of a triangle are together equal to two right angles is a truth to all intelligences, is a truth to God. That love is good, that cruelty is bad, is in like manner a principle which approves itself to all moral beings, and, we must believe, to God Himself. We must hold that the promotion of moral good and the discouragement of sin is an ultimate end with Deity.

QUESTIONS.

INTRODUCTION.

SECT.
I. 1. PHILOSOPHICAL inquiry and practical knowledge presuppose? 2. What do we expect in the material world? Do we expect the same in human affairs? 3. Our knowledge of the laws of nature is obtained? How far does it extend? 4. What is the business of philosophy? Who first pointed this out? What did the ancients seek? To what mistakes did it lead? 5. The object of philosophic inquiry is the same with? The advantage of the practical knowledge of events? 6. Wherein does philosophic knowledge differ from it? What process is dignified with the name of *Philosophy?* 7. How far does our knowledge of the course of nature extend? This happens when? But in most cases the actual state of things is? In such how can the result be predicted? 8. The first step in philosophy? What may we afterwards do? These processes are respectively called? Define them. 9. The method is called? We owe to it? For what are we indebted to Bacon?

II. 10. Has the method been as successfully extended to other branches as to physics? This appears? The evil may be corrected? 11. Our knowledge of the mind rests on? What may we expect from an examination of the facts of consciousness? Whose writings furnish examples? 12. The objections against inductive mental science are similar to what? To what is the business of philosophy confined? Researches on mental and material science terminate in?

III. 13. Specify some of the chief causes of the slow progress of human knowledge? Show how some of them apply more specially to the mental sciences?

Subject and Arrangement.

1. The object of Moral Philosophy? 2. The inquiries may be arranged under three heads? 3. The two first coincide with? Why should the third be also embraced? 4. A fourth topic might be introduced?

Part I.—The Intellectual Powers.

SECT.

What is Stewart's enumeration of these? 5. Are those named common to the whole species? What other capacities may be considered? How are they formed? Mention some of them. An interesting subject of inquiry? 6. Certain auxiliary faculties are essential to our intellectual improvement?

I. 7. Define CONSCIOUSNESS. 8. How does it stand in reference to the present operations of the mind? 9. What is the character of the belief attending it? What other beliefs are similar to it? 10. We cannot be said to be conscious of what? Which comes when? 11. From Consciousness and Memory we acquire?

II. Art. I. 12. The SENSES are commonly reckoned as five? An attempt has been made to resolve them into one? What is said of it? 13. TOUCH and TASTE differ from the others? 14. Define Sensation and Perception? 15. The *Qualities* perceived by SMELLING, TASTING, and HEARING, are known to us as? They have been called? They are distinguished from? Which are known how? Name some of the latter. 16. The Senses named could give us no information about? 17. But what might they suggest? 18. TOUCH is spread over? What makes the hand its most important organ? 19. There is a distinction in the qualities perceived by Touch? But in all its perceptions there is a common circumstance? What seems to arise from this? 20. How is the hand useful? What paradoxical opinion has been held about it? 21. What does this organ intimate? and refute? 22. SIGHT. How is the picture formed on the retina of the eye? What science inquires into this? But what has mental science to do here? 23. There is a distinction between the *original* and *acquired* perceptions of this sense? What do we perceive by it prior to experience? We may reach other perceptions? how? 24. The distinction explains what? Proves what? 25. Mention two other questions concerning vision, and say what they illustrate. 26. Some qualities perceived by sight are *primary?* Others *secondary?* 27. Mention some instances of the general accommodation of our animal frame to our intellectual faculties.

II. Art. II. PERCEPTION. 28. Our notions of body and mind are said to be *relative?* 29. How are we led to consider body and mind as distinct objects? How are we to study each? 30. What can we ascertain concerning the connection between mind and body? 31. What knowledge have we of *secondary* qualities? What by sensation? What by philosophical investigation? The names of such qualities are ambiguous? Hence the paradox? 32. The *primary* qualities are apprehended as? What relation have they to the sensations which suggest them? 33. Our sensations having no resemblance to external qualities have given rise to a difficulty? and to scepticism? 34. What was the ancient theory of perception? The images since the time of Descartes have been called? And the hypothesis? 35. What consequences did Berkeley draw from the theory? By what argument? 36. The reasoning is conclusive, on what admission? What objections are taken to the Ideal Theory? 37. Who first called it in question? What account does Reid give of our belief in the material world? 38. What is Leibnitz's theory as to the communication between mind and matter. 39. Certain general laws have been ascertained as to perceptions. 40. But we are ignorant of?

III. ATTENTION. 41. From what does it appear that there may be processes of thought which are forgotten next moment? What seems necessary in order to fix thoughts and perceptions in the memory? This power is called? 42. We may employ the fact, how?

IV. 43. Define CONCEPTION. 44. Are the objects of all the senses conceived with equal ease? 45. Is conception accompanied with a belief in the existence of its objects? 46. What proves that the faculty has an intimate connection with the body?

V. ABSTRACTION. 47. Our perceptive powers make us acquainted with? Does this comprehend the greater number of the subjects of thought? 48. The process of classification involves? By what power accomplished? Define Abstraction. 49. Define generic words? They enable us? The best illustration of the use of signs in reasoning? Misunderstandings long prevailed in regard to general terms? 50. What renders us capable of general reasoning? A branch of Logic is recommended? 51. We must guard against another error besides the ascertaining the truth of general principles? Another branch of Logic is suggested? 52. Certain extremes are to be avoided?

VI. 53. What is meant by the ASSOCIATION OF IDEAS? 54. Enumerate some of the circumstances which regulate the succession of our thoughts? Which is the most powerful of the associating principles? 55. Mention an important distinction among these. Specify the relations under each head? What does the distinction account for? 56. Is the train of operation regulated by the will? Has the will any influence? 57. Can we summon a particular thought before it appear? What can the will do directly? 58. The will has an indirect influence? 59. Give illustrations of the strengthening of particular associating principles. 60. What evil effects may be traced to education? It may be turned to good purposes by education?

VII. 61. Certain theories of MEMORY are hypothetical? 62. What proves that Memory depends much on the state of the body? 63. In what way may we account for differences of Memory? 64, 65. Whence the varieties of Memory? What the constituents of a perfect Memory?

VIII. 66. The province of IMAGINATION? 67. It results from a combination of faculties? 68. In what most clearly exemplified? What its influence in human affairs?

IX. 69. How is JUDGMENT defined by logicians? 70. A distinction between two kinds? Hence between two kinds of Evidence?

I. 71. *Intuitive Evidence* comprehended under three heads? Give examples of fundamental laws of belief. Mention some characteristics of such truths. 72. This class has been called? What vagueness is there in the expression *Common Sense?*

II. 73. Intuition is implied in Reasoning? 74. Locke distinguishes between Intuition and Reasoning. 75. What criticism is offered? 76. Admitting Locke's account to be just, what faculties may be shown to be identical? 77. The power of reasoning is implied in intuition and memory? In syllogism the mind proceeds, how? What is argued from this as to the truth of the conclusion being perceived before the formation of the major proposition? 78. Distinguish between two kinds of *Deductive* Evidence. 79. What is the process called Invention? 80. Two sorts of Logic are mentioned? What is said of each?

X. 81. Whence the varieties of intellectual character? 82. Give examples of the intellectual differences produced by different pursuits? 83. An examination of the effects of different occupations would suggest? 84. What phrases express important characteristics of intellect? 85. Certain inquiries open a curious field of inquiry? Such an inquiry lessens? 86. Is Taste considered an original faculty? 87. What must it have in the original qualities of the mind? Yet it is the result of what? What gives it the appearance of an immediate perception? It is analogous to?

XI. 88. The form and posture of the body have a fitness? Certain auxiliary powers specially promote man's improvement?

SECT.

I. 89. We are indebted to artificial signs for? 90. Artificial LANGUAGE pre-supposes, according to Reid, certain natural signs? 91. There is a dispute as to the interpretation of the expressions of the countenance? 92. How do natural and artificial signs stand towards each other historically? 93. Artificial signs are divided? Which class forms the ordinary medium of intellectual communication? 94. Some writers have traced the parts of speech and the progress of language to? 95. The imperfection of popular languages has suggested an idea? 96, 97. The advantages of the arts of writing and printing?

II. 98. How does IMITATION show itself? 99. It has advantages? 100. When is it strongest? Who avail themselves of the natural tendency? 101. What phenomena may be explained by it?

XII. 102. BRUTES regulate their conduct in a different way from men? 103. How is Instinct distinguished from Reason? 104. Instinct indicates Divine Intelligence? 105. Which is most conspicuously exhibited in certain instincts? 106. Animals can make acquisitions? 107, 108. Theories have been formed by French philosophers as to the difference between man and brutes? 109. In what respects does our nature not admit of comparison with that of the lower animals?

PART II.—THE ACTIVE AND MORAL POWERS.

110. How is this Part divided?

CHAP. I.—CLASSIFICATION OF OUR ACTIVE AND MORAL POWERS.

I. 111. The word *Action* is properly applied to? In what sense is it used in ordinary discourse? In what in this treatise? 112. The primary sources of our activity? Those which make part of our constitution are called? Enumerate some of them? To what heads may they be referred?

II. 113. By what circumstances are our APPETITES distinguished? 114. What their number? What are they respectively intended for? Could reason accomplish these purposes? 115. Why cannot they be called selfish? When is self-love sacrificed to appetite? 116. Name some acquired appetites. What follows the stimulating of the nervous system? 117. There are propensities analogous to the appetites?

OUTLINES OF MORAL PHILOSOPHY. 151

SECT.
III. 118. How are our DESIRES distinguished from our Appetites? 119. Mention the most remarkable of our natural Desires.
    I. 120. The DESIRE OF KNOWLEDGE appears in children? It is commonly proportioned to what? What direction does it take as we advance in years? The Desire is different in different individuals? What is its final cause? 121. It may be shown not to be a selfish principle by specifying its object, which is?
    II. 122. There is a DESIRE OF SOCIETY abstracted from what? To what does it lead us? In whom may we see it? 123. What contributes to strengthen it? This has led some authors to do what? What is certain independent of any speculative question? 124. In what may we see how powerfully this principle operates? 125. Show how the Desire of Society and the Desire of Knowledge co-operate. A provision is thus made for what?
    III. 126. How does the DESIRE OF ESTEEM show itself in infants? What is meant when it is said to be an original principle? It can be shown to be a native Desire? What difficulty is there in the way of accounting for it by the association of ideas? 127. Is it a benevolent principle? But what does it subserve?
    IV. 128. How does the DESIRE OF POWER manifest itself generally? 129. It is exhibited by the infant and the boy? 130. How as we advance in years? It may be seen in the orator? 131. And in the pleasure arising from the discovery of general theorems? It comes to aid another instinctive Desire? 132. What part has it in our attachment to property? 133. What account is given of avarice? What strengthens it? 134. The love of liberty can be shown to proceed in part from the Desire of Power? 135. Show how Cicero resolves the love of tranquillity into this principle? 136. What influence may it exercise on the pleasure of virtue?
    V. 137. The DESIRE OF SUPERIORITY is a Desire rather than an Affection? 138. There may be emulation where there is no malevolent affection? 139. Butler distinguishes between emulation and envy? 140. Does it operate among the lower animals? To what extent among men? 141. What constitutes artificial desires? Mention some. What have they been called? What principle explains their origin?
V. 142. What are comprehended under AFFECTIONS? Mention some. They are distinguished as?
    I. 143. Mention the more important BENEVOLENT AFFECTIONS. 144. Are they all original principles? Some of

them may be resolved into? But they are all This may be illustrated by what like mental phenomenon? 145. What is said of the question of the origin of the affections? There is another question more important? 146. In what order might the affections be treated in a course of lectures? What follows applies to? 147. With what is the exercise of all kind affections accompanied? Who avail themselves of this? Tragedy derives its principal charm from? There is a question started by this fact? 148. With what do the pleasures of kind affection mingle? A misleading influence is thereby produced? 149. Is the feeling altogether painful when the affections are disappointed of their objects? 150. The final cause of the agreeable feeling should induce us? 151. The pleasure arising from the benevolent affections does not show them to be selfish? 152. The preservation of the individual and the continuation of the species entrusted to something else besides self-love and reason? The acquisition of knowledge to something else besides self-love and benevolence? Our sense of duty is strengthened by? What affections acting independently of reflection promote social union?

II. 153. What are the names given to the MALEVOLENT AFFECTIONS in common discourse? There seems, however, to be only one such principle naturally in the mind? How are the others grafted on? 154. Resentment is distinguished as? How does Instinctive Resentment operate? What does it guard us against? When does it cease? 155. Deliberate Resentment is excited by? What does it imply? 156. What is Indignation? What seems the final cause of Deliberate Resentment? 157. The malevolent affections are accompanied by? 158. What does the word *Passion* apply to? The effects of passion? Mention some mental affections that may be called passions. The word is commonly applied to?

V. SELF-LOVE. 159. The nature of man is analogous to that of the brutes in respect of? What renders him essentially different? 160. The brutes are incapable of? But man is able to? This implies? 161. A man's character receives certain denominations? According to what? What makes his conduct systematical? 162. What effect has a steadiness in the pursuit of a particular end? 163. An exception is specified? What is said of the performances of vain men? 164. What influence has systematic conduct on happiness? 165. In respect of seeking happiness, man differs in one important respect from the brutes? 166. Wherein does the desire of happiness differ from the principles of action hitherto considered? 167. Self-love as a title of the section is exceptionable? The similarity between self-love and selfishness has introduced? 168. The word *selfishness* being always used in an unfavourable sense has led some authors to suppose? We apply the epithet *selfish* to? but not to? 169. Show how the word selfishness when applied to a pursuit has reference to the *effect* and not the *motive*. 170. Show farther how selfishness is not synonymous with a regard to our own happiness.

VI. MORAL FACULTY. Art. I. 171. What have some philosophers been led to conclude concerning virtue? What has led them to do so? Wherein may the two principles of rational self-love and virtue be said to coincide? 172. What is the 1st circumstance that shows that a sense of duty cannot be resolved into a regard to happiness? What the 2nd circumstance? What emotions particularly show this? And why? What is the 3rd circumstance? How is the truth reached that a virtuous life is true wisdom? What is the 4th circumstance? 173. It has been alleged in order to elude the force of these considerations? What seems to confirm this allegation? 174. Answer this by showing that education proceeds upon and presupposes certain natural principles. 175. Education in diversifying the appearances of human nature depends on? And this supposes? 176. What can education do, and what can it not do, in regard to our sentiments of beauty and virtue? 177. We must make allowance for what in looking at the historical facts in regard to man's moral judgments? 178. To what length have some licentious moralists gone? 179. What affords a sufficient refutation? 180. The licentious moralists have confounded? Admitting the depravity in the world, what proves that we are formed for the admiration of moral excellence?

Art. II. 181. What question comes next to that of the universality of MORAL PERCEPTIONS? What various opinions have been formed on this subject? In order to form a judgment we should look to? What three things are we conscious of as we do so?

I. 182. The controversy in regard to the ORIGIN OF OUR MORAL IDEAS arose from whose writings? What were the views expounded by Hobbes as to our approbation of virtue, and the ultimate standard of morality? 183. What did Cudworth show in opposition? To what did he refer the origin of our ideas of Right and Wrong? 184. How are we to understand him when he makes reason distinguish between good and evil? 185. What did Locke's Essay introduce? With what defect is that Essay charged? What is Locke's doctrine as to the origin of our ideas? 186. Into what dangerous opinions did this system lead him as to moral distinctions? Can his conclusions be avoided on his system? 187. For what purpose were certain theories proposed? Specify one of these? What was done in all the theories? 188. What was Hutcheson's doctrine as to the origin of our moral ideas? What his general doctrine as to the materials of our judging, and the province of the intellect? 189. What are our perceptions of right and wrong according to this system? 190. Sceptical conclusions were drawn from this hypothesis of a moral sense by certain writers? What did these conclusions make morality? 191. What doctrine did Price expound in opposition? 192. Whence the obscurity involved in the discussion of this question? 193. Moral distinctions may be perceived by a sense, provided what be granted? 194. What was unfortunate in Hutcheson's illustrations? But sceptical consequences do not follow, provided we look on moral perceptions as analogous to? 195. What suggested the word *Sense* to Hutcheson? What objections may be taken to his definition of a Sense? May the word be retained in ethical science? 196. What then is the doctrine of Price as to the origin of moral ideas? and as to the understanding being a source of new ideas? 197. The controversy chiefly turns on? The origin of our ideas of right and wrong is the same with that of certain other ideas? It is essential that the words Right and Wrong express what? 198. What are the various senses in which the word Reason is used? In what sense is it used in common discourse? and by those who refer moral ideas to it? What do their antagonists understand by it? May we distinguish between reason and reasoning? How should we understand *reason* when moral ideas are ascribed to it? 199. Mention some intuitive judgments involving simple ideas. Are the judgments and ideas to be referred to different powers? May we ascribe the origin of certain ideas to reason? 200. What is the main truth to be attended to? What should we mean when we say of a particular act that it is right? There is an analogy between mathematical and moral truth? Can scepticism as to these be met by argument? 201. Some philosophers have called in question the essential character of duty from pious motives? What follows if we deny the immutability of moral distinctions?

II. 202. Show that every good action must be a source of pleasure to the spectator. Other AGREEABLE FEELINGS

| SECT. | come to be associated with virtuous conduct? 203. The qualities in good actions which excite agreeable feelings are called? 204. Those which excite disagreeable feelings in bad actions are called? 205. What two things are to be distinguished in moral actions? What consequences have followed from looking exclusively to the one or other? 206. The exquisiteness of the moral emotions has led to a theory of beauty and sublimity? 207. What are the most delightful of all objects to the human mind? 208. How may we add to the natural beauty of virtue?

III. 209. What do virtuous actions excite towards the agents besides the pleasurable feeling? Unfold fully what is involved in the perception of MERIT in others? 210. And what is in the sense of DEMERIT? A good end is served by this impulse of mind? 211. What do we feel in regard to ourselves when we are conscious of doing well? 212. And what when we have done ill? 213. Between what two things has God established a connection? The most direct road to happiness? But are good and bad fortune always connected with good and bad actions? The vulgar fall into mistakes on this subject? How does the philosopher feel?

VI. Art. III. 214. What question is put to those who maintain that MORAL OBLIGATION arises from the command of God? Only two answers can be given? Examine the answer, that there is a moral fitness that we should conform to the will of God. 215. What conclusions follow from the system that we are led to obey God from prudence? 216. The notions of reward and punishment presuppose? 217. The strongest argument for a future state? What difficulties are they involved in who found moral obligation on a regard to our situation? 218. What answer is given to the question, Why are we bound to practise virtue? What does every one who knows the distinction between right and wrong carry about with him? What, according to Butler, renders obnoxious to punishment? 219. Show how the moral faculty differs widely from the other powers. 220. Who did not pay sufficient attention to the supremacy of conscience? Who is represented as establishing this doctrine? 221. What is the important question in ethics? in regard to the origin of moral ideas? or what? What does A. Smith say as to our moral faculties?

VII. 222. Mention some principles AUXILIARY TO VIRTUE. What has led some authors to confound them with our moral powers or to suppose that they can account for moral perception?

SECT.

I. 223. What does DECENCY or a REGARD TO CHARACTER proceed from? What influence does it exert? 224. But what considerations show that our sense of duty cannot be resolved into a desire of esteem?

II. 225. Describe SYMPATHY as shown by others to us, and by ourselves to others. Into what might it be resolved in such cases? 226. How is the word applied in a loose sense? 227. Are the different phenomena thus included under the word sympathy the same? What is needed when philosophic precision is aimed at? 228, 229. What is the merit and what the error of A. Smith on this subject?

III. 230. What is the proper object of RIDICULE? 231. Good ends may be served by it? 232. What place has it in our constitution and our world?

IV. 233. What is represented as subserving the gratification of TASTE? 234. What is said of the culture of moral taste? 235. What good ends may it promote? When and how may it prove a fallacious guide? 236. Into what errors have certain philosophers fallen?

237. When may unfortunate consequences flow from the above principles? And when good results? 238. What has a partial consideration led to?

VIII. FREE AGENCY. 239. The foregoing inquiries all suppose? This supposition is agreeable to? 240. An opposite opinion has been held, by whom? How has their argument been proposed? 241. What is the first form of the Necessitarian system? What is said of it? 242. It has been admitted on the other system? What interest attaches to the discussion? 243. Scepticism has proceeded, from what source? 244. What is professedly done in this treatise?

CHAP. II.—THE VARIOUS BRANCHES OF DUTY.

245. The different theories of virtue have proceeded from? 246. What arrangement of Duties is adopted?

I. 247. OUR DUTIES TO GOD are inferred from? An examination must be undertaken in consequence? What is said of such an examination?

Art. I. 248. Two modes of reasoning have been adopted to establish the EXISTENCE OF GOD? 249. The *a priori* argument is enforced by whom? It seems to have been suggested by what? State the argument of Clarke. And also Reid's judgment upon it. 250. What is said of the argument *a posteriori*? 251. Is the existence of God an Intuitive truth. What is required in order to present its full force? What are the premises of the argument? Whence derived?

SECT.
I. CAUSE AND EFFECT. 252. Whence our knowledge of the course of nature? We cannot perceive a connection between two events such as? 253. What objection has Hume deduced from this principle? 254. What is his general doctrine as to the derivation of our ideas? How does he show that we have no such idea as power? What relation does he allow between cause and effect? 255, 256. Upon the doctrine of Hume (and of Locke) it is not possible to explain? 257. Are we entitled to reject the idea because we cannot refer it to the senses? There are two expressions not the same in import? Unfold fully the two considerations urged to show that we have an idea of power different from succession. What sort of conviction have we on the perception of a change? 258. What is said of the inquiry as to the origin of the idea of causation? 259. What is the most probable account? A power of beginning motion is an attribute of? 260. A conclusion may be drawn as to the Divine power? 261. State the various hypotheses which have been devised to avoid this. 262. What is said of them? What is the doctrine which they oppose? It is said of that doctrine? 263. What sort of powers do the phenomena of the universe indicate?

II. 264. What is said of the phrase FINAL CAUSE? 265. Reid represents the argument from final cause as having two premises? These denied by whom? 266. Hume denies? 267. What account does Reid give of the inference from design? 268. What other objection is taken? 269. Mention three considerations which may be urged in reply? 270. Two other inquiries remain? 271. What prospect does advancing science hold out as to these? 272. What satisfactory illustrations does the universe furnish of the wisdom and unity of God? Various adaptations are specially mentioned? 273, 274. Certain relations between the nature of man and his situation are peculiarly striking? 275. Mention some curious analogies illustrative of unity of design. 276. How far does uniformity of plan extend? The views on this subject in modern, are different from those in ancient times? 277. What have we reason to suspect as to the arrangements in the different planets? 278. Specify instances of uniformity in the moral world. These give a charm to? 279. What view is to be taken of the metaphysical reasonings employed? 280. What is necessary in order to worthy conceptions of the Divine Attributes? What follows when attention is confined to isolated appearances? 281. What view did Descartes take of the argument from final cause? Who replied to him? 282. What account is given of

OUTLINES OF MORAL PHILOSOPHY.

SECT.

Bacon's views on this subject? 283. It is not necessary now to banish final cause from physics provided? In what branch has final cause been an instrument of discovery? An instance is specified? 284. An addition to logic is suggested?

I. Art. II. MORAL ATTRIBUTES. 285. The Divine power and wisdom are said to be *infinite*, how is this explained? The Divine attributes are commonly divided into? What two attributes are to be treated of?

I. 286. Whence our ideas of the moral attributes? 287. Whence our conviction of the DIVINE BENEVOLENCE? 288. Without the *a priori* presumption what opposite views might we take of the mixed phenomena of the universe? 289. What furnishes an answer to the objections urged against the Divine benevolence? 290. But what impression might be left if we had nothing else to consider? What are we led to inquire? 291. Enumerate some of the theories which solve the origin of evil? 292. There is one derived from the doctrine of pre-existence? What is said of it? 293. What is that of the Manicheans? How is it refuted? 294. What is the fundamental principle of the Optimists? 295. This theory takes two forms? What is the first form, and who are its supporters? 296. What the second form? 297. What evil has arisen from confounding the two forms? 298. Distinguish between Moral and Physical evils? 299. What is the question in regard to the former? What the reply? 300. The sufferings produced by vice on this supposition are? 301. These observations justify many physical evils? 302. Some other complaints arise from? 303. But evils remain to which these principles do not apply, such as? 304. Show how this class is to be explained? 305. Good effects arise from "time and chance" influencing human affairs? 306. There are moral qualities fostered by physical evils? 307. What appears from all this as to partial evils? 308. What is the relation of the sum of happiness to the sum of misery? 309. It has been insisted on in opposition? 310. Can any objection be drawn from the state of the fact, whatever it be, to the foregoing reasonings? How is it shown that the proportion of human life spent in vice is inconsiderable? 311. Show that the argument is made still clearer by the tendency of general laws. 312. A number of occasional evils may be traced to? 313. Certain special pleasures illustrate the Divine goodness? 314. What beneficial influence is exercised by habits? 315. What leads us to form too low an estimate of the happiness of life?

I. II. MORAL GOVERNMENT. 316. The strongest proof

SECT.
of the moral attributes of God is derived from? 317. The distinction between right and wrong apprehended as? What, therefore, are we entitled to argue from our moral judgments? 318. What do our sense of obligation, and our sense of rectitude, imply? 319. There are other sentiments which point to a moral administration? 320. The examination of the course of human affairs, shows the great object of general laws to be? The disorders in the world point to?

I. Art. III. 321. The consideration of the Divine attributes, and man's moral constitution seem to require what as a sequel? Show that a FUTURE STATE is implied in every system of religion. But that the truths of religion are not necessarily implied in the doctrine of a future state.

I. 322. What may be legitimately argued from the soul's IMMATERIALITY as to its Immortality? 323. Show that it is involved in our conceptions of Mind and Matter, that mind is not material. 324. What leads us to habits of inattention to the distinction between Mind and Matter? 325. What is fitted to cure a tendency to materialism? 326. How does it come that materialism seems less absurd than the system which represents *Mind* as the only existence? Yet that system is the more philosophical, why? We have *no* instance of what? 327. State the argument for the existence of mind derived from what is suggested by every change, and the combination of means to an end. 328. Is the union of soul and body essential to the exercise of our faculties? It seems rather intended to? In reflecting on the difference between mind and body we are led to suppose? 329. What are the most plausible objections to the doctrine of a future state? 330. What is Cicero's reply? What the remark made upon it? 331. These conclusions might be supported by?

II. 332. Enumerate the principal evidences for a future state, derived from MAN'S CONSTITUTION AND POSITION? 333. What is the force of these arguments taken singly? What when taken in conjunction? 334. Show that all the doctrines of Natural Religion hang together. 335. And that they have a relation to the other principles of Moral Philosophy. 336. A confirmation of these remarks is added? 337. What influence has the belief in a future state on the conduct and enjoyments? What has this led some to suppose? What is urged in opposition? 338. What DUTY TOWARDS GOD arises from the evidences of his perfections in his works? 339. In what way should we feel towards God? 340. Is religion the sole foundation of morality?

But the conviction of an infinitely good God should lead us to? 341. What ought to conspire with other motives to virtuous exertions? Our moral perceptions indicate? What then may religion be considered? Extending over what? What view of religion secures a discharge of duty among the lower orders? 342. A sense of religion leads to resignation?

II. 343. What is proposed to do in regard to OUR DUTIES TO OUR FELLOW CREATURES? With what special view? Can virtue be resolved into any one principle?

Art. I. BENEVOLENCE. 344. It has been supposed by some moralists? 345. What would follow from the doctrine that merit depended entirely on the amount of good intended? What are acknowledged to be virtues by the universal judgments of mankind. 346. If these duties are not immediately obligatory what would follow? 347. It may be urged in opposition? What reply is given to this objection? 348. What is allowed as to the utility of virtues? And as to what *may be* the sole principle of action in the Deity? But what is affirmed with respect to man? 349. What do the moral systems objected to agree in? Of what older doctrine are they modifications? 350. What however is said of the duty of Benevolence? 351. Define Benevolence? It is not to be confounded with? What is said of kind affections? 352. What do the epithets *virtuous* and *vicious* properly belong to? 353. What influence would a settled benevolence have on the conduct? Mention some expressions of benevolence?

Art. II. 354. Define JUSTICE? 355. What should we do in order to free ourselves from the influence of bias? 356. For what intention? Into what error has A. Smith fallen? 357. Specify two of the more important effects of Justice. What may these be called?

I. 358. CANDOUR may be considered in three points of view? 359. Whence the difficulty of estimating candidly the talents of others? What should a good man endeavour? What when outstripped by others? 360. Whence the greater part of the disputes among mankind? What should we do in judging of the intentions of others? 361. Candour in Controversy implies two qualities? How do these respectively manifest themselves? They are difficult of attainment? What so far secures them? 362. Is Justice the same as Honesty. What account is given of honesty?

II. 363. Explain what is meant by UPRIGHTNESS or INTEGRITY? Who drew distinctions between Justice and the other virtues? To what do they apply? 364 Two circumstances chiefly distinguish Justice from the other virtues? 365. What other distinction is insisted on by Hume? 366. What is his principal argument? 367. How is it shown that Benevolence and Justice as virtues are on precisely the same footing? The propriety of our conduct does not depend on affection, but on what? 368. Certain implanted principles imply a sense of Justice? 369. Show how the natural impulse to Gratitude is an additional means of keeping alive the obligations of Justice. Gratitude is a branch of Justice, and a branch of Benevolence? The casuistical questions on this subject do not occasion any hesitation when? A reflection is offered as to the various parts of our constitution? 370. What do the rules of Justice admit of? The part of Ethics which treats of them is called? 371. What has it copied from the Roman code? 372. What influence has this had on the science of Jurisprudence? 373. And on other branches of Moral Philosophy? In what branch of virtue have we Right and corresponding Obligation? What fictions have been employed to find the same and other virtues? 374. In what are Justice and Utility closely blended? This has led Hume to remark? With what should jurisprudence be united? This would illustrate the general principles of Justice and Expediency as combined in what?

Art. III. 375. What would follow if no foundation were laid for VERACITY in our constitution? 376. There are other grounds of the approbation of this virtue? What does Hutcheson speak of? 377. What place has the principle of veracity in our nature? 378. What account is given of faith in testimony? It bears a striking resemblance to? 379. Which of these is the more conspicuous in infancy? What hinders the manifestation of the faith in testimony? 380. What do breaches of veracity indicate? What does sincerity combine? 381. Under what head should fidelity to promises be ranged? 382. When a person fails in the execution of a promise which he meant to perform, what is his fault? 383. When a person promises, not intending to perform, what is he guilty of? Does a declaration of present intention amount to a promise? But what does every promise involve? 384. The practice of veracity is secured by certain maxims? Besides insincerity in speech veracity prohibits? 385. To what else does the same disposition lead? What account is given of the Love of Truth? 386. Point out the close connection between error and misery, truth and happiness? 387. Name some other duties arising from the particular relation between us and other men.

SECT.
III. Art. I. DUTIES TO OURSELVES. 388, 389. What duties are mentioned? Why placed under this head? 390. On what account are they and the habits which lead to them approved? 391. Another duty is recommended as leading to the practice of all the rest?

Art. II. 392. What is the doctrine of Hutcheson as to moral approveableness of self-love, and a regard to the pleasures of a good conscience? 393. What is said of self-love in the text? 394. The inferior principles of our nature interfere with what? 395. In such cases what judgment do spectators, and we ourselves when the passion is over, pronounce on our conduct? 396. Why is our indignation against the neglect of private good not so great as against social crimes? 397. What view does one who believes in a future state take of a bad action? 398. In what circumstances might a man disregard the prohibition of the civil magistrate? In other circumstances what would such a disregard be?

Art. III. 399. Can happiness be obtained by gratifying every appetite? In order to secure it what must we form? 400. There have been discussions as to the system to be preferred?

I. 401. The opinions of the Ancients as to the Sovereign Good may be reduced to three? 402. What is the doctrine of Epicurus as to pleasure, and pain, and virtue? 403. Whence the pleasures and pains of the mind according to his system? What pleasures are of most value? In what did he place the supreme good? 404. On what account does the system deserve to be studied? 405. In what did the Stoics place the supreme good? 406. What was the Stoic doctrine as to objects of choice and rejection? For what end were objects to be chosen or rejected? When we have done our utmost how should we look on the event? 407. What was the Stoic scale of desirable objects? How were events ordered according to this sect? How should this lead to an entire acquiescence in Divine Providence? 408. Acknowledging the weaknesses of humanity, how did they justify their exhibition of a lofty standard? 409. Wherein did the Peripatetics agree with, and wherein did they differ from, the Stoics? 410. What did all the sects acknowledge? What peculiar views did the Stoics maintain?

II. 411. What is the sound view of the dependence of happiness on external circumstances on the one hand, and on the mind on the other? 412. Mention some limitations of the high Stoical doctrine? 413. Mention some mental qualities, having no moral desert in themselves, which are necessary to insure happiness? 414. Through these the mind may be influenced by? And when this is the case what is to be done? 415. What is meant by Temper? How is it connected with happiness? 416. What is deliberate resentment? 417. An irascible temper results from? In whom is it most frequently observed? 418. What is necessary to keep up animal resentment? This indicates? From what must this disposition proceed? 419. How may these mental disorders be cured? 420. What may help to suppress their violence? This proceeds on what law of the connection of mind and body? 421. The causes which alienate our hearts from our fellow creatures produce other evil results? 422. Show that temper and our views of the administration of the universe reciprocally influence each other. 423. Mention one of the principal effects of a liberal education. Show how this enlarges the sphere of our enjoyment or suffering. 424, 425. Wherein do men differ as to the pleasure or pain proceeding from the Imagination? 426. What delight does it furnish to those fortunately educated? 427. On what does the character of our imaginations depend? 428, 429. In particular what is the influence of association of ideas? How may these associations be guided and corrected? 430. What is meant by Opinions when they are said to influence Happiness? 431. How are a large portion received? 432. When these are erroneous how are they to be corrected? What is a special duty devolving on those capable of reflection? Where is this subject illustrated? 433. What was previously said of the effects of Habit? 434. What evils may arise from these? 435. To what should the minds of children be habituated? 436. What pursuits should we choose? When we have done so what will Habit do? 437, 438. The essentials of happiness being secured, what will the sum of happiness be proportioned to? 439. Under what heads may the pleasures belonging to our nature be ranged? 440, 441. What is said of the examination of these classes of enjoyments? 442. What is the practical conclusion resulting from the whole inquiry? 443. Show that though there is a connection between happiness and virtue, yet that the principle of duty is different from the desire of happiness. 444. Show how the desire of happiness as a guiding principle is inferior to the sense of duty.

IV. 445. Whence the different theories of virtue? 446. Whence their plausibility? 447. What good has sprung from their being started? What is shown by the circumstance that so many consequences may be traced from distinct principles?

SECT.
V. 448. The various duties have one common quality? And are enjoined by one authority? Are articles of one law, called? 449. What does moral excellence denote? Who may be denominated virtuous? What is the oldest definition of virtue? 450. Explain what is meant in the statement of Aristotle, that where there is self-denial there is no virtue?

VI. 451. There is an ambiguity in the epithets virtuous and vicious? 452. A distinction was introduced to obviate the confusion thence arising? 453. When may an action be said to be absolutely right? 454. And when relatively right? 455. According to these definitions an action may be? 456. What does relative rectitude determine? What absolute rectitude? When may utility be affirmed to be a quality of virtue? 457. What will a strong sense of duty induce us to do? Is it our duty to do what appears right at the time? If in doing this we incur blame, whence the demerit? 458. When are actions meritorious?

VII. 459. When is it specially necessary to employ reason in the regulation of our conduct? 460. How does the study of happiness become an important part of Ethics? 461. Where has the subject of happiness, as relating to the individual, been considered? Where must the subject as relating to the happiness of the community be considered? 462. In what other respects, besides their relation to happiness, are politics connected with other branches of Moral Philosophy?

THE END.

JOHN CHILDS AND SON, PRINTERS.

www.ingramcontent.com/pod-product-compliance
Lightning Source LLC
Chambersburg PA
CBHW020258170426
43202CB00008B/420